Breaking Through

From Rough to Ready

by

Karim Abouelnaga

Copyright © 2018 Karim Abouelnaga. All rights reserved.

No portion of this work, in part or in the whole, may be copied, duplicated, broadcast, or otherwise transmitted without the written permission of the author.

All circumstances and personalities described or contained in this work are the product of the invention of the author. Any similarity to persons living or deceased is wholly coincidental.

ISBN-13: 978-1-7323620-0-0

First Edition

Printed in the United States of America

Set in Calibri 11 point.

Practice Makes Perfect Holdings PBC

www.practicemakesperfect.org

What's Being Said About...

Breaking Through: From Rough to Ready

- Karim's incredible journey is a testament of perseverance and his unwavering dedication of soul searching and success while overcoming incredible odds is something we can all learn and grow from. – Damien Hall, Clinical Researcher

- Karim's story is both heart-wrenching and uplifting. His triumph from jail to CEO is a testament to those inner-city youths that where you start is not as important as where you finish. This is a must read for all high school students! 10 Stars! – Naphtali T. Bryant

- Karim's story is a blend of rawness and inspiration! REAL life struggle of a minority who rises from the level of stealing and excels to Cornell, is by far a path not often found but should be emulated. – Susan Tanner, Associate Director, Moody's Analytics

- The book is amazing! It's a riveting story that's easy to fall into. – Stephen Reese

- Wow, this is a page turner! Any young person facing adversity will be inspired to overcome their personal barriers. - Keisha Alexander a Americorps College Coach at Anderson County High School in Kentucky

- I'm blown away by the insights and the hustle. I wish I had read something like this in high school. – Progga Choudhuri, College Student, City College of New York

- Every lesson is a lesson to prepare you for your next breakthrough. – Tony T. Alexander, SPHR, Managing Director at SGI Services

- Truth be told to succeed in our world is hard, but it if you grind and keep this book as your bible you will find your way through. – Julien Mouyeket, Operations Manager at Taxify France

- Karim's book is a story on how to use your struggles to fuel your success. Karim provides numerous nuggets of priceless advice I wish I were exposed to when I was in high school. Any young person will highly benefit from reading this story. – Veronica Canton, JD Candidate, University of Notre Dame

- This book provides an inspiring message for those seeking success. As a millennial leader and a pioneer in education, Karim is at the forefront of understanding the socioeconomic circumstances that can often dissuade people from reaching their full potential and greater success. – Greg Weatherford II, Millennial Entrepreneur & Higher Education Executive

- After only reading through half of chapter two, I sent up this little prayer: "Thank you, God, for sending Karim to us." – Ellen Yui, Founding Principal, YUI+Company, and author, "Selling Your Soul"

- Karim's story is inspiring to anyone - across age, race, sex, or walks of life - that has ever experienced hardship and feared an inability to overcome and thrive. – Tyler Shine, Manager, Investment Analysis & Valuation at MGM Resorts International

- A book for those inner-city kids that think they don't have a chance of leaving the hood. A book that sheds light on bridging social capital. – Yesenia Peralta, Teacher, New York City Department of Education

- Those of you who have an inward feeling that your life can be more than what it seems to be...please take advantage of similar and other opportunities he did, knowing that your life matters! – Elizabeth Ngonzi, NYU Adjunct Faculty

- This book belongs in a must-read list for those students who are looking to be inspired and who want to understand why getting an education and going to college is the best way to discover their life's purpose. – Jorge Perdomo, Principal, New York City Department of Education

- So real and so raw! It's a phenomenally easy read that inspires you - to learn from and look past life's struggles and attain that end goal. – Raj Gujar, Management Consultant, KPMG

- Each page is mind-blowing, each lesson so simple but powerful, each part of Karim's story touching and honestly analyzed. – Francois Khan, Studies Coordinator for Parkours and Consultant specialized in Education for "Together for Human Development", a French NGO

- Relatable, honest and quite simply an addictive read. I highly recommend other students pick it up. - Ridhwan Haque, Student at University College London

- *Breaking Through* includes the foundational building blocks for a successful life. It doesn't matter where you're from or what you've been through, you have inside of you what it takes to create an incredible life! Karim's story demonstrates this beautifully. Now, it's your time! - Clarence Lee, Jr. MD, MBA, Former USAF Flight Surgeon, CEO of PERSIST Institute, & Author of *PERSIST*

- Karim shares a painfully honest narrative of personal heroism and achievement in the face of deep-seated systemic barriers. His writing is raw and penetrating even as it inspires and uplifts. - Joshua Mbanusi, Former educator and social justice advocate

- This is THE book I wish I would have read in high school, the time I wanted to embark on my entrepreneurial journey but found no support. – Muhammad Malik, Founder at Speekr UK

- This book is a blueprint for minority children who want to be successful in a world that has intentional barriers. – Luis Torres, Principal and Chairperson of the Bronx Elementary Schools Principals Consortium, New York City Department of Education

- This is a must-read for students, educators, parents, counselors, and businesspeople alike, as its message is clear – anyone can achieve anything. – Charlie Clausner, Teach for America Educator – Hawaii, Johns Hopkins University – Masters of Educational Studies

- Powerful and deeply personal, Karim's book "Breaking Through: From Rough to Ready" touched me with stories of Karim's strength and vulnerability, inspired me with his vision and courage, and has shown that though his talent and tenacity, he has become a change agent for thousands trying to find their authentic self. – Russ Watts, Executive & Organizational Consultant

- Karim has written the blueprint for young people to build a successful foundation in their personal and professional lives. I wish someone gave me this book and forced me to read it when I was younger as it would have saved me years of pain and confusion. – Mahmoud Khedr, City College of New York

- A must-read, for all of us! This book is a wonderful human journey, full of inspiration, mind and heart opening thoughts and ideas, brilliantly written and narrated by Karim. It is an odd to life, to success and to greatness. – Reda TALEB, CEO Officium Morocco

- Karim's honest and heartfelt story is one that uplifts and encourages all of us to do better and be better, and his insights inspire us to achieve more than we ever imagined. - Wendy M. Lau, Partner, Wood Smith Henning & Berman, LLP

- This book will fill you up. You will be propelled toward righteous action. You will pay it forward. – Jordan Stockdale, Former Harlem middle school teacher

- Trust in oneself is the super power Karim possesses as he moves us through the beliefs, thoughts and behavior throughout his life. When the world showed him pain and cruelty, he showed the world brilliance and the deep intrinsic conviction in oneself because – all our lives matter. – Monique Betty, Executive Coach

- Every leader ought to add this book to their library. Karim expresses the type of vulnerability it takes to be an impactful leader in today's world. – Mason Singer, CEO, Unboxd, INC.

Dedication

To my mentors who have taken the time to invest in me and my future. In many ways, this book is a byproduct of your wisdom, guidance, and love.

To our partners at Practice Makes Perfect who give me the honor and the privilege of working with their children.

Table of Contents

Preface	13
Introduction	17
Lesson 1: Education Can Save Your Life	51
Lesson 2: Trust the Right Adults	61
Lesson 3: Ask for Help	67
Lesson 4: The Secret to Success is Less, Not More	73
Lesson 5: Understand the Rules of Society and Play by Them Sooner	79
Lesson 6: Define Your Legacy and Go with the Flow	89
Lesson 7: Money does not Solve the Root Causes of Family Problems	95
Lesson 8: You Cannot Choose Your Family, but You Can Choose Your Friends	103
Lesson 9: Your Attitude and Perception Can Dictate Your Reality	109
Lesson 10: My Secret to Happiness	113
Lesson 11: Eliminate Self Doubt	119
Lesson 12: Delay Gratification and Think Long Term	127
Lesson 13: Follow Up	133
Lesson 14: Do Not Dwell on Rejection	137
Lesson 15: Workplace Etiquette	141

Lesson 16: Hacking the College and Career Application Process — 147

Conclusion — 153

Preface

This book was inspired by my siblings. It is dedicated to all the kids who were not born into the "one percent" of supposedly privileged human beings, but who want to achieve economic mobility and lasting self-worth.

This book is for every kid who has ever been lost and wants to be found, every kid who has ever been told they wouldn't amount to much but doesn't believe it, every kid who has struggled in school and felt like they couldn't learn, every kid who was forgotten, every kid who has ever been bullied in school, but didn't trust the adults to handle the situation, and every kid who has been given almost every reason not to have hope, but has not given up yet.

If you're reading or listening to this book, this moment can be an opportunity for hope. Your life matters and you're capable of so much more than you probably believe. I'll focus on my life story because I was like you. I changed my situation for the better—and so can you.

These lessons were written with you in mind. I don't pretend to know the full impact that I want to have on our planet yet, but I'm sure of one thing. I've achieved more than I ever thought possible. I feel an obligation to share with you the lessons that have been given to me.

As I start writing this book, I'm 25-years-old and I run a multi-million-dollar education company that I started when I was 18-years-old. The last seven years of my life have been a blessing. I've traveled to a dozen countries, met a former United States President, attended two Ivy League universities, raised millions of dollars, networked with a handful of billionaires, interned at some of the most elite companies in the world, and have discovered my life's purpose to create equitable educational opportunities for kids growing up just like me.

For those experiences, I am eternally grateful to God, my mentors, family, and friends. But I didn't start here. The lessons throughout these pages are my attempt at sharing the wisdom responsible for my success. Many of these lessons may sound familiar, but were just "words." I ask you to take these lessons from someone who has walked in your steps, and I invite you to walk in my steps, letting my life story be a testament to what is possible for you.

Are we alike? I didn't read my first book until I was in the fourth grade. After that, I did not read my next full book until I was in my second or third year of high school. The fact that I'm now publishing books feels unreal to me. My grade school teachers wouldn't believe it.

Writing to you in this book is especially challenging for me because I am committed to telling you the truth. That includes telling you about my home life—a story that doesn't cast my parents in the best light. But I want my honesty to give you confidence that your home life isn't hopeless, no matter how bad it may seem at times.

Let me be honest about writing to you in this book: it has been a painful process. It brought back to mind so many early childhood memories that I've chosen to just black out for many years. I often tell people that you could not pay me enough money to live the first 18 years of my life over again.

I have lived years of my life as if those difficult years of growing up never happened. Thinking (and feeling) about what I went through didn't make me feel great about my adolescence, my environment, or the way my siblings and I were treated by our parents. I often heard my parents say they regretted the day we were born. They probably thought of us as holding them back from the life they could have had.

I could have waited to write this book, as many people advised, but somehow I knew you were waiting to read it. I didn't want time to erode my vivid memories of how bad things can be— and my discovery of my power, and your power, to turn things around. I feel I'm breaking through my past, shedding the rough parts, and getting ready for what lies ahead.

I invite you to come along on this journey with me, beginning with my first faltering steps.

Introduction

Learn from yesterday, live for today, hope for tomorrow.

- Albert Einstein

I was born on December 15, 1991 to two Egyptian immigrants at Jamaica hospital in Queens, New York. I came a year after my older brother Moez and a year before my younger brother Monzer. The three of us would eventually become seven. I was told we lived in one of my father's friend's attics my first couple of years.

My father moved to the United States after dropping out of high school in Egypt. In every sense of the word, he was a natural born hustler. When we were kids, I remember him telling us about how he would catch pigeons and sell them to his friends. He never excelled in school; he figured that he could just get some kind of job and make enough money to get by. Nonetheless, he was my first mentor and role model.

My mother wasn't much better off. She was one of a dozen kids only able to finish high school in Egypt. Her father had a furniture business back home that she used to work at before she decided to join the workforce to delay getting married. My mother told me she got married relatively later than all of her sisters. I guess she was waiting to meet my father.

After a few years in the United States, my father went back to Egypt and met my mother. That's when they started their lives, and my journey in the United States.

Knowing what being poor feels like

Like most immigrants, my parents came to the United States with very little, and not just in the financial sense. From conversations I had with my mom, I learned that my parents did not really have a plan for how things were going to work out. They were literally living day to day. My father's work was inconsistent, sometimes by his own fault and sometimes by others. The original plan for keeping a roof over our heads was to stay with friends, no matter how cramped the conditions were.

The details on when that kind of living would end were never ironed out by my parents. They were full of half-baked ideas for a better future, but things never seemed to work out. There were always obstacles they hadn't foreseen. As you can imagine, not having money created a lot of strain on their marriage, which translated into perpetual arguments and anger.

For my entire childhood, we struggled with money. Before I started high school, my family moved at least six times—and not because we were "moving up." Most of the time, we had to move because we were behind on our rent. Often landlords got so sick of my parents' excuses and delays that they would give us a month of free rent just to get us out.

Moving sucked for me. Every single time it meant having to start over, trying to make new friends, learning the "rules" of a new neighborhood, and just finding different ways to pass time.

Looking for reasons

Like many immigrants, my parents were poor with below average education. For many, that's an unpromising and compromising combination. When we were kids, it seemed like every day there was new drama or an emergency that would stress our parents out. Most days, the stress would lead to arguments and oftentimes, the anger would be taken out verbally and physically on me and my brothers.

I lost count of how many times I just wanted to run away from home. The abuse from my parents got so bad that in many instances I just wanted to take my own life. That's a terrible thing to admit, I know—but it's true. I could not stand the constant arguing, the physical abuse, and the endless repetition of it all.

To this day, I remember making a promise to myself that I would never lay an angry hand on my kids. The experiences I had as a kid were nothing short of traumatic. My parents said they were "teaching me." I can't explain what meaningful life lessons I was supposed to take away from those beatings.

One thing, however, became clear: our parents were raising us to fear them instead of raising us to respect them. That important difference truly impacted how we felt and treated them as they got older, and we became of age.

Family tragedy as a mixed blessing

When I was 14, my father was diagnosed with lymphoma (a deadly form of cancer). Right around that time, things had started to change in the daily routine of anger and beatings. My older brother had grown tall and strong, bigger than my mother. When she would attempt to strike him out of anger over some infraction or lack of respect, he would fight back.

The same happened with our dad: he couldn't physically abuse us without consequences, especially as his cancer treatment gradually debilitated him. The combination of chemotherapy and radiation took a huge toll on him. Within the span of 11 months, my father was on his deathbed and passed away in February of 2007.

As painful as it is for me to write this, my life actually became a little more tolerable after my dad died. Now, we only had one "enemy" to deal with—our mom. It was only a matter of time before we all acted out against her in one way or another. Although I hate admitting it, our father's death felt like a moment of liberation.

Not to say that my father was all bad. He was caught up in problems he couldn't handle, a marriage that brought more anger than joy, and eventually a disease that killed him. Despite the many faults, in my father's best moments, he gave us a glimpse of what he could have been like. In fact, my success as an entrepreneur today was largely fueled by watching him get excited about new ideas and having him support some of my entrepreneurial pursuits as a kid.

For example, when I was 12, I designed a heated pad toilet seat. My dad took me to the Invention Submission Corporation and we had an entire feasibility analysis done on the idea. Right around that same time, he funded an online course for me that taught me HTML and allowed me to start an online business. It never got any traction, but the experience was influential. From his decision to support my entrepreneurial desire, I grasped that my dad really did care about how his kids turned out.

Making it on our own

Our parents' inability to support us meant that we had to fend for ourselves. My brothers and I did everything we could to make money and get the new Air Force One's or Jordan sneakers that we wanted—the ordinary things that most of our friends seemed to receive from their parents without asking. We sold candy on school nights and weekends. We picked cans and bottles out of the garbage and recycled them at the local supermarkets.

We even went as far as stealing the things we wanted. We knew it wasn't right. Initially, we did it only to get the things we needed, like sandwiches from the supermarket so we didn't go hungry. Then, the habit of "borrowing and not returning" started to transcend our needs for food. I found myself stealing hundreds of dollars in football equipment before the season started and even more in clothes on Black Friday. Our mom didn't think much of it since we had jobs.

Like many of you reading this book, we turned to the streets for love, friendship, and encouragement that we did not have at home. Of course, we learned how to steal and not get caught by following the lead of the older kids we meet at the park and the ones who lived on our block.

In retrospect, I feel lucky to have my siblings. I'm the second oldest of seven. The first three of us are just one year apart, so we all grew up together. We were each other's first friends. When we went into new schools, which happened often, we went together. We always had someone to go with to the park. And my siblings were always a ready audience to complain to about our parents and how much we hated something that they did to one or all of us. Life with siblings wasn't always peachy, of course. There were the times when our fights inside the household spilled into the streets. Our friends would join in, literally helping us beat each other up. For the most part, having siblings to go through the first 18 years of my life made a huge difference. I can't imagine my early life without my siblings.

Getting a job

My brothers and I have been working in one way or another since we were five years old. I worked in the family business moving boxes and selling souvenirs, as a waiter with a traveling catering company, as an intern in a school food kitchen, as a lifeguard, swim instructor, customer service representative, and janitor at an aquatic center all before I got college.

My father first worked as a taxi driver. By the time I was five, he had gotten into an accident that provided him with a bit of insurance money that he used to start importing souvenirs from Egypt. He would sell these at a premium in flea markets across New York City. Since we couldn't afford to hire help, my mother was his first employee. That meant my brothers and I would be among the lower-level hires in this make-shift family business.

I hated the flea markets as a kid. We always had to wake up at 6 am on the weekends when our friends were sleeping. There were times when it was raining and cold; all we wanted to do was stay home and go play basketball at the park with our friends. But that was not an option—we had to go to the flea market.

My father invested the money he made from the flea markets in a thrift shop in Manhattan. One would think that owning a business was the epitome of fulfilling the American Dream, but I thought it was one of the worst things that could have happened in my life. This meant that we would not only have to help on the weekends, but we'd also work after school. We moved tables; we cleaned souvenirs; we swept the front of the shop, all while our friends were having fun at the parks, hanging out, or just sleeping. I later grew to appreciate the work ethic. These early experiences shaped me. From an early age, I knew what it meant to do what I had to do, not just what I wanted to do.

Troubles with the law

My first experience with the police was when my father thought it was a clever idea to buy knockoff or fake designer bags and watches to sell to tourists. He was arrested a handful of times trying to make a quick buck the easy way. By the time I was ten, my father moved his thrift shop to a bigger location in midtown Manhattan. By then, my siblings and I became pretty good salespeople. We knew how to negotiate and give customers "deals" to sell them more merchandise than they meant to buy when they entered the store.

At the same time, my father also had another surprise for our family. He announced that he was marrying a second women. In Egypt, it might have been common, but in the United States, it was the first time I had heard of such a thing. Apparently, he had to legally divorce my mom to make this second marriage happen.

Needless to say, my mother would never agree to something like that. So, he forged her signature on the necessary legal documents. For months, I remember seeing my mother broken in body and spirit. She went through swings of being depressed and being enraged, and, of course, my brothers and I got the short end of all her raw emotions. By the time my brothers and I were teens, we become numb to her verbal abuse. The only thing that would pierce our skin was her nails when she would scratch us. The swings she would take at us with her fists didn't hurt and we would dodge the objects she would throw at us.

A combination of poor planning and business upsets one day pushed my father over the edge. Before he discovered he had cancer, he already had a less visible illness. In the year or so leading up to his diagnosis, he had become a full-time gambler. He was barely home. He lived in Atlantic City where he was losing a lot of his money, my mom's money and any other money he could get his hands on. I would watch how he would manipulate everyone around him to get a few dollars to go to the casinos—and then lose it all.

Then he did the unthinkable. Through his business, he started illegally charging people's credit cards for thousands of dollars in merchandise they never bought. My father always found a way of convincing us that doing these illegal things was never really that bad. I remember him justifying this by saying that the money he took would be given back to the people by the banks.

So, he reasoned, at the end of the day, he was taking the money from the banks. Since the banks had so much money, they could afford to lose it. I don't know how much money he took, but I know it was substantial. It was also short-sighted. His actions would impact our entire family and how our extended family and friends in Egypt would view us. Not to mention, he would take the money, gamble it, and lose. My dad wasn't smart with money.

He did this a few times before he realized he would get caught very soon if he kept it up. That is when he told us he was going to gather a huge amount of money and flee the country to Egypt where we would start a new life and later bring us over to join him.

I think I was in seventh grade at the time. I did not really understand what it meant, but I remember telling my friends about how I was moving to Egypt. Within a few months, my father was back from Egypt. He somehow found a way in Egypt to gamble away all the money he fled with from the United States.

When he got back, he told us how he attempted to commit suicide and failed. He realized he had nothing in Egypt and came back to live with us. At this point in his life, his second wife had abandoned him. When he went on his gambling spree, he chased the people who were closest to him away. He had cheated most of his closest friends in one way or another. My mother told us if it were not for the five boys she had with him that she would have left him as well. She felt trapped. Her English language proficiency was still very limited, despite being in the country for fifteen years at that point. She had few options but to keep living a life she hated.

Even when my father was alive, he was often a poor role model for us. When his second marriage started, he would alternate the days he spent with us at our home and with the new family he was building with his second wife. Sharing my father with another family felt weird. It did not help that I did not like my father's second wife because of the pain she caused my mother. Despite the pain my mother caused, she was my mother. I wanted to love her. I was taught that I was supposed to love my mother unconditionally and that she would love me unconditionally.

Knowing what I know now, it is hard to hold anything against her. My father was looking for something more and should share equally in the blame. Besides, I love my two siblings that he had with his second wife. I was grateful to reconnect with them almost eight years after he passed away.

Months after, when my father returned from Egypt, the FBI quickly came for him. His credit card scheme involved at least one felony, if not more. He was on his way to serving serious time in jail before they found out he had terminal lymphoma. I would like to think that my father knew he had cancer long before he broke the news to us. Maybe his gambling habits were his attempt to leave our family with some money—at least I would like to believe that. After all, he had seven children who ranged in age from one to fifteen years old. He did not have any life insurance and his business was deeply in debt. Our family would be left with nothing in his absence, but his mess to clean up.

Of course, the drama in my life did not end there. After a year or so of my father's passing, my mother started to date again. She was looking for someone to help her raise her boys. After all, we were more than any one person could handle. My brothers and I felt like her dating ambitions came too soon. We told her we would continue to give her hell if she even thought of remarrying in the short-term.

It was shortsighted. For some strange reason, we felt a social obligation to our father. Despite all that he did, including marrying a second wife over my mother, we felt that our mother's remarrying would be like cheating on him. And he was dead. We had to protect him and what was left of his reputation. Even though I struggled to rationalize the poor decisions my father made, I wanted to remember him for the good he did. Besides, the idea of our mother dating was weird to us.

My brothers and I did a good job of sabotaging her efforts. Every time my mother would get close to sealing a deal, we would find a way to scare the person away. Probably the worst incident was when one guy gave her an ultimatum. He told her it was him or the oldest kids, meaning he would marry her and help take care of the younger boys, but there would be no way in hell he would even consider marrying her with the three teenagers. My mother did not successfully remarry until my older brother had moved out and I was in college.

It is no wonder my brothers and I were acting out. Our household was unstable. We did not have adults we could turn to or look up to at home. Our teenage years were probably as close to hell as possible for our mom. Immediately after my father passed away, my mom found out that she had a slipped disc in her lower back. She did not qualify for disability, and she was rendered incapable of doing any job that required lifting things or standing for extended periods of time. Her limited English also meant that she could not get a secretarial job. Besides, who would look after my one-year-old baby brother if she did find a job? A babysitter in most cases would cost her more than she could make with her limited education and limited English language proficiency.

Our mother's inability to support us meant that we could do whatever we wanted. A parent missing-in-action was not right, but we did not know any better. We were working and paying most of the rent. We worked and bought our own clothes. We worked, and paid our phone bills. After my father passed away, my mother cooked less and less for us. I realize now that we were living as independent young adults from the time we were fifteen.

My life was a constant struggle. I did well in school in the primary grades, although now I know that academic expectations for me were not very high. I also had the luxury of following in the shadow of my older brother and getting many of the teachers who were so frustrated with him. He consistently acted out in class. When teachers got me the following year, they thought I was an angel. I thrived off this contrast, at least until I got to middle school.

My older brother and I went to different middle schools. Right around that time, I started to disengage from school. I was struggling in my classes and I didn't really my teachers or the other kids in my classes. I had over sixty absences when I was in seventh grade. I just didn't feel like going to school. I would just stay in my bed until 10 am and then wake up and have a huge bowl of cereal as I watched the morning game shows. My parents had us working late nights in the store and we all believed that one day we would be taking over the family business. The best education we could get to one day take over the family business would be best provided through more hours in the store. My father did not finish school and he had a store, so why did we have to finish school?

We were convinced that school was useless. My mom would make half-hearted attempts to wake us up for school every day, but she ultimately left the decision to us—at least until we got to high school and the government threatened to cut off her public assistance if we did not go to school.

I still remember my seventh-grade teacher offering to throw the entire class a party if I showed up to school for a week straight. So, I showed up for a week straight during the week of my birthday and she threw a party. I do not remember doing very well in school until high school. Nonetheless, I always got better grades than my brothers. As a result, my parents would rarely be called in for meetings with my teachers.

I was much smaller than the kids in my grade all the way through my senior year of high school. I was the easiest target for bullies. Naturally, I hung out with the other kids who got bullied. They happened to be the kids who were bullied for doing well in school. In many ways, they saved me from a dead-end life. By their standards, there was nothing wrong with getting A's and B's.

When I was 13, an endocrinologist discovered that I was Human Growth Hormone (HGH) deficient. My pituitary gland wasn't creating HGH levels that it was supposed to produce. The doctor succeeded in persuading my mother that I needed treatment. For almost four years, I injected myself with a daily dose of HGH to bring my HGH levels to normal. From the moment I started this treatment to the time I finished, I grew over a foot and gained over 60 pounds.

The beginning of the turnaround

Despite not going to school for more than a third of the year in seventh grade, by the time I was in eighth grade I thought I could be just as smart as the kids I was hanging out with. I've always had this innate desire to be the best – even when I was far from it. I decided, I would take the specialized high school admission test like many of the eighth graders in the city and try my luck at getting into Stuyvesant or Brooklyn Tech, both highly desirable high schools.

By the time I wrapped up eighth grade, I had spent enough time with the smarter kids in my classes to start to *care* about my grades. A couple of them liked me enough to let me copy their homework and reference their tests to make sure I got the right answers too. I wish I could say this was strategic, but it wasn't. The smart kids were the ones who seemed to be most accepting of me. I spent my entire childhood just trying to find a group of people to belong to.

When the results of the exam came out, I was devastated. I did not score even close to the range I needed to be admitted to any of the specialized high schools. As a result of my poor attendance, after middle school, I enrolled in my local high school, Long Island City High School, which was one of my only options. People referred to the school as LIC or Lesbians In Charge. LIC for short, Lesbians In Charge because there were a lot of openly gay girls who were thought to run the school. By then, my father had lost the store and it was clear we were going to have to find another way for ourselves to overcome our situation.

There were 4,400 students there when I started my freshman year. The school's graduation rate when I was a freshman was 55 percent. When it came time for me to graduate, there were only 526 students in my graduating class out of the over 1,000 students who entered in 2005 with me. Among the 526 students that graduated only 20 percent were "college-ready" based on the CollegeBoard assessments. An even smaller percentage went on to four-year colleges.

Because I did well in eighth grade, the high school put me on the honors course track. It just meant the kids I would be taking classes with were better behaved than the kids in the other classes. That would give me a chance to learn. Kids were in honors classes because of their behavior and not because of their aptitude.

I was surprised to find myself interested in high school. I figured I would keep doing well in school because I finally realized that I enjoyed excelling in school from my eighth-grade experience. I thought that maybe I could be the smart kid who helps my friends with their homework and tests, much like my friends did for me in middle school. By then, my father had passed away, the family store no longer existed, which meant that there were no demands imposed on me and any of my siblings by the family business. I was finally in control of my life and all of my time.

Throughout high school, I had a wide variety of odd jobs. I worked as a waiter, a lifeguard, a customer service representative, a janitor, and a swim instructor. I sold candy for a couple of years, I worked in school food kitchens in the summers and did any job so I could make sure I wasn't dependent on anyone else. I also had the added responsibility of paying a large portion of the rent to keep my family from living in the streets.

The independence that was created by the jobs my brothers and I had, and the money we earned, led my brothers and me to do whatever we wanted. Never again did we really need my mother's approval for anything. That meant we would stay out as long as we wanted, whenever we wanted. We brought visitors over to the house, which was something we were never allowed to do as kids, and we disobeyed our mother's prohibition against us visiting other people's homes.

By time we were 13-years-old we started drinking, smoked occasionally, played basketball in the park all hours of the day and we got into fights in the streets. One day, the kids I grew up with started going around and randomly punching people in the face. To this day, I cannot tell you why we did it. I knew it was wrong, but I did not want to be the one to stick out from the group. It was peer-pressure at its finest.

We were becoming the typical inner-city kids that everyone was afraid of. We felt like we had nothing to lose. It took me a few years before I gave up shoplifting completely. Though I started to earn money, I inherited a mindset from my father in which it was okay to take from big businesses like Macy's because they would not really feel the impact. That meant free shopping sprees on Black Friday when there were way too many people at the shopping centers for any store to notice anyone who was shoplifting.

Before high school ended, I watched my older brother get arrested a few times for doing the wrong thing and by being in the wrong place at the wrong time. The sad part about it all was that we thought it was cool to get arrested and come out of jail with stories to share. Where I grew up, it was. I smoked my first joint when I was a sophomore in high school, not because I wanted to try it, but because I wanted to fit in – even if it meant doing the wrong thing.

I was on the football team for three years in high school. I still remember walking into the bathroom at a catering hall that my football coach rented out for the entire team to celebrate our city championship my sophomore year when I ran into two of the seniors who told me it was my lucky day. I believed them. I smoked with them and I thought I was cool. After the getting over the fear of smoking, I became desensitized to all of the negative things people would say about smoking. Luckily, it never became a habit for me.

I can't point to one moment in time where everything turned around at one time for me. In fact, it was a series of events over time and a set of intentional decisions I made that helped me break out of this dead-end life I was well on my way to leading. One of those lucky breaks came at the end of my sophomore year of high school. I had just wrapped up taking an Advanced Placement (AP) course in European History when my high school was selected to participate in an incentive program called Rewarding Achievement (REACH) that was going to pay kids to pass AP exams – as much as $1,000 to pass one exam. I was incredibly excited before my AP European History exam score came out. I committed to taking three AP courses the following year. That was a huge 180-degree turn from where I was a year earlier when I was begging my guidance counselor to get me *out* of AP classes.

I was getting 90s and 95s in European History on homework assignments and exams. Then I was told I only needed to get above 50 percent of the AP exam right to receive college credit, which was a score of three out of five. When the score for the AP exam finally came out, I learned that I scored a one out of five, which was the lowest you could possibly score on the exam. Originally, I thought the College Board made a mistake. Today, based on what I know about our public schools and system, I am glad I did not embarrass myself by asking for a re-grade.

Thankfully, the REACH program also flew the best AP instructors from all around the United States into Baruch College for supplemental workshops on Saturdays to help us pass the AP exams. By the time I graduated from high school, I had passed five AP exams. In hindsight, I know that my ability, and the ability of so many kids growing up just like me, is a product of a resource-deprived environment and some lack of intelligence as some researchers would like us to believe.

At the last payout session, I remember approaching Eddie Rodriguez, who was the Executive Director of REACH at the time, and thanking him. The money I received did not feel right immediately. I had friends who were attending other struggling schools who were working just as hard to pass AP exams and they were not being rewarded for them as I was. Although it was not a direct handout, I felt like it was. I was skeptical. I felt that by taking the money, I would have to pay it back. But once it was spent, there would be no telling how long it would take me to make a few thousand dollars again.

Nonetheless, I went up to Eddie and I thanked him. I asked him if there was anything I could do for him, and he replied "pay it forward." That was Rewarding Achievement's slogan. It meant that the way we would pay it back or make good on what we were given would be to help someone else.

To this day, paying it forward is at the core of my values. I took what Eddie asked me to do to heart. I figured that if I could pay it forward, then I would be paying him back. I also thought that it would be cool to one day have the kind of impact Eddie had on my life on the lives of other kids growing up just like me.

The AP classes I was taking and the exams I was passing made me feel smart. I was managing the workload in addition to working almost 40 hours per week. From the moment I joined the football team as a sophomore in college, I was labeled the "smart one." In most inner-city neighborhoods, you didn't want to be smart. The smart kids would get picked on. That was the case in my high school, too. For some reason, I dodged all of that. I think a large part of that was because I played football.

I did what the smarter kids in my middle school did for me. I shared my homework answers and allowed my friends to check their answers against my test answers. I knew I was cheating, but I would watch what happened to the kids who did not help when they had the answers – and it was not good. I also did not understand why we all had to do the same exact work independently when we were supposed to be a team and help each other out.

I am not condoning cheating, but I am condoning survival. If adults are giving you a hard time about wanting to survive, then they obviously do not understand what's at stake. In hindsight, it did not do my friends much good to cheat. They did not learn the material on their own and they probably struggled with it again after high school. To this day, I regret not being strong enough to do more to help them – especially knowing what I know now about our messed-up school system.

The college decision

When it came time to apply for college, I was convinced I needed to leave home. My junior year I heard about a program called QuestBridge. I applied for their junior summer intensive program, but I did not get in. Since I did not get into a specialized high school when I was in middle school, I looked upon this as my second big failure or setback as it related to school. I thought QuestBridge was going to be the break that I needed to get out of the hood. When I got to college, I realized that I probably wrote at the level of a seventh or eighth grader at best. I never mastered the fundamentals of grammar and I had a limited vocabulary. I can only imagine how basic my personal statement for college was today.

Right before school started, QuestBridge had a consolation prize for everyone who did not qualify for the intensive program. They would be invited to a regional summit. I was one of the ones who received the consolation prize. The summit one I went to was at Yale. I learned more about their application process for college and I started to think about the application I was going to put together.

After a few meetings with my college counselor, I decided I was going to apply to and get into Massachusetts Institute of Technology (MIT). My college counselor thought it was a bad idea. She thought it was a reach school for me. I did not believe her. I learned about the school on the movie *Goodwill Hunting* in which Matt Damon played the role of a janitor who solved math problems at night. I thought MIT was the school I wanted to go to. My college counselor was a State University of New York (SUNY) Albany alum and she thought that was a good school for me. She figured I had the scores and the narrative to likely get in there.

I didn't like the fact that my college counselor did not believe in my chances. After all, I was one of the smartest kids in my high school. Against her advice, I applied to two schools: MIT and the local city college known for business, Baruch College. I applied to Baruch's prestigious Macaulay Honors program. I figured if I didn't get into MIT, then I was a shoo-in for Baruch's honor program.

In the fall of my senior year, I went to visit MIT during one of their prospective student weekends. I bought a $15 bus ticket from Chinatown and took a six-hour ride to Boston. It was my first time going to Boston and also my first time being that far from my family on my own. I was anxious. The buildings on MIT's campus looked like they were straight out of a Dr. Seuss book. So many of them looked wacky and fun.

After my visit, I was sold. My only regret is that I did not get the help I probably needed with my personal statements to truly convey my journey and what I had been through. After overcoming my childhood, I was certain nothing anyone threw in my way could stop me. If passing five AP exams with moderate support and subpar living conditions was not a miraculous endeavor that would qualify me for any school in the nation, then I did not know what was.

I knew tuition would be expensive if I got into MIT. Plus, there were things that financial aid did not cover, like books and travel to see my family. I applied for dozens of scholarships. I would search the internet for scholarships and write down the deadlines and the submission requirements and go through my list to apply to them one by one. When the list got shorter, I would go and search for more scholarships. Often, I would get home from work at 9 pm or 10 pm., then wrap up my homework by midnight and work on scholarships up until 2 am.

My mother did not understand why I wanted to go away for college. She thought I just wanted to get away from everything and run away from the responsibility of paying rent, providing for food, and having to watch my younger siblings. There was definitely some truth in that. But then again, she was not confined in an 80-square-foot room with two other people like I was. She also did not know the difference between any of the schools, nor did she care enough to find out. She did not believe I would leave.

Just as college applications were due, I had a friend convince me to submit a last second application to the University of Pennsylvania. It was an Ivy League school in Philadelphia that kids who wanted to study business went to. I think I received my rejection letter from the University of Pennsylvania first. Shortly thereafter, I found out that I was not admitted to the Macaulay Honors program at Baruch, but I would be invited to enroll in the traditional honors program. It was a significantly watered-down version of the Macaulay program, but it was better than nothing.

At the time I found out, it did not matter. I was sure I would be going to MIT anyway. I thought I would be receiving my acceptance notification soon.

Then, on what MIT coined as national Pi day (3.14159), they released the decisions online. March 14th at 1:59 pm. I remember being at a Rewarding Achievement workshop when I rushed to one of the Baruch computers to get my notification that I was accepted. Nothing else would matter.

Waiting at the computer at 2 pm that day was the longest hours of my life. The rejection notification broke me. Not only did I have my heart set on getting into MIT, I had told everyone in my school that it was the college I applied to and was going to.

I do not remember having anyone to really turn to. My mother was rooting against me. The rejection meant I'd be staying in the city for my first year of college. I had friends, but I did not have any who really cared about my college future as much as I did. Most of my friends did not turn in their college applications. The last thing they could be bothered with was my MIT decision. There were more important things. Besides, they thought I'd get in, too. I was one of the smartest people they knew.

"Your attitude determines your altitude" was the platitude written on the sixth-floor hallway at my high school. Within a week or so, the disappointment turned into motivation. How could MIT reject me? I remember making a commitment to myself to get the best grades at Baruch and be the most successful person I could be to prove MIT wrong.

It was silly. In hindsight, my SAT score may have ranked me in the 95th percentile in my high school, but I was only in the 70th percentile nationally. MIT was recruiting kids with SAT scores in the 90th percentile and higher nationally. They assumed I might not have been able to keep up if I was admitted. I am sure there were a lot of other compelling applicants who had support presenting themselves. Nonetheless, the MIT rejection was the third largest failure I had experienced, at least in my own view.

New possibilities and old obstacles

Luckily, it wasn't all bad news. The honors program at Baruch meant I would get a full ride, tuition free. Then, many of the local scholarships started to roll in. I could not compete on a national level given my SAT scores, but I still stood out on a local level. I started winning scholarships that would give me some discretionary money going into my freshman year of college. The checks started coming to my apartment and I shared the news with my entire family. It was probably annoying to my siblings.

My mom's first reaction to seeing that kind of money was to ask me for more support with the rent and the bills. At the time, I was paying $300 - $400 a month, which was about one-fifth of our rent expenses. My older brother and my brother who was just a year younger would chip in too, collectively contributing between $1,000 - $1,200 per month. We made most of our money selling candy and working as lifeguards at a local aquatic center.

When I told my mom that I would not be able to chip in more money to support, she got angry. I told her the money was for college and books. She did not understand. Instead, she said she would pray to God that I did not get any more scholarships since I was being so selfish with my scholarship money. It was an uncomfortable feeling. As a teenager, my relationship with my mom was always rocky. The lack of respect was probably mutual.

When my father passed away, she also decided to become very religious. Her version of religion seemed weird to me and I did not want much to do with it. We practiced a few religious rituals when our dad was around, but it was never forced on us in the way my mother was trying to force her religion down our throats after he passed away.

When the next scholarship check came in the mail, I waved it in her face to let her know her prayers went unanswered. With what felt like all her might, she cocked her hand back and smacked me across the face.

She was angry. I could not believe it. To this very day, I do not know that I have completely forgiven my mom for that moment. I did not talk to her for at least three months. I remember not wanting her to even show up to my high school graduation. She did not come.

How could my own mother be angry at me in one of my proudest moments? When she smacked me across my face, I felt like our relationship hit an all-time low. The role that I always envisioned a mother would play did not describe the woman I was living with. She never came to my parent-teacher conferences; she did not come to any of my sports games; she was not at my senior awards night – all of which I excused because she had other priorities. But her physical abuse at the moment of my best scholastic fortune to date was a new low—one I couldn't just forgive. To this day, I haven't been able to forget it.

That experience rivaled only my 16th and 17th birthdays when I came home and she asked me in front of all of my siblings where the cake was. I was the first one not to get a cake for his birthday. My mom usually found a way to spare a few dollars to get a cheese cake or go to the supermarket to buy a cake that would cost her less than five dollars to make. I remember not talking to her for a period of time after those confrontations as well.

As a kid, I did not learn how to cope with all of my emotions. When I would get upset at something, I would shut down and run to my bed for the night. Often, my retreat was on an empty stomach with tears streaming down my face. I thought I was making a statement, but no one really cared.

When I got older, I would just shut people out of my life for periods of time. I did it to my mom; I did it to my brothers; I even did it in my early relationships with women. I think a large part of it was to avoid being like my father. When he got angry, he would lash out, many times breaking things or unleashing his temper on us physically. I wanted nothing to do with his style of emotional release. Frankly, it scared me.

Today, I know that the healthiest way is to deal with my emotions head on. If it is a person I am upset with, I need to talk to that person directly. I realized that holding grudges only weighed me down. Lacking direct contact, I would always have that thought in the back of my head that there was someone I needed to avoid or not deal with. That kind of emotional drag was unnecessary. I know now that I don't want to devote time, energy, and anxiety to matters that can be settled quickly.

I graduated from high school when I was 17. I had a late birthday that worked in my favor. Right around that time, I had friends who were getting cars either from their parents or through some hustle. The guys who had the cars naturally picked up the cuter girls.

Naturally, I wanted a car too. My older brother and I graduated from high school at the very same time. He immediately signed up to get his driver's license. I followed suit. Just as we were nearing the summer, my older brother passed his road test. On my first attempt, I failed. The next road test was weeks away.

That summer, my mother decided she was going to return to Egypt to reconnect with family she had not seen in years. She was going to take the two younger boys, but she was going to leave the rest of us at home by ourselves. We had no relatives or anyone to look after us. She made an occasional call to make sure we had not burned the apartment down.

Since my older brother had just passed his road test, she decided to leave her car in his hands. I begged her to buy me a car before she left. I had saved up enough money for a down payment and I had a reliable source of income to be able to keep up with the monthly payments and insurance. I told her it would make getting to and from work easier for me.

Her first response was a quick no. Then it became a "maybe, if you pass the road test." I failed. There was no way she was going to help me buy a car before she left. Without her name on the insurance, I would be paying a hefty premium because of my young age. My only consolation was once I got my license I could share the car with my older brother.

Within a few weeks, I had crashed my mom's car twice. In both cases, the accidents involved parked objects and I was able to get the car to a repair shop for touch-ups. Unless someone snitched, she would never find out.

That's when my need for a car got a little more interesting. I started to search for ways to buy my own car. I had saved about $3,000, which seemed enough to get me a decent car off Craigslist. After a week or so of searching, my older brother and I finally found a car that looked suitable. It was a 2000 Chrysler 300M. We reached out to the owner and arranged for a time to meet up.

The seller told me that there were a few things that needed fixing, but they all seemed trivial. In hindsight, I should have gotten the car inspected. It was one of the most expensive lessons I ever learned as a teenager. At the time when money was scarce, I had to replace the radiator, the entire front windshield, the muffler, and eventually the engine. Thank God for the scholarship checks I received to buy books, because I spent every dollar in my savings to keep my car running.

The only thing the seller gave us was the title to the car. He did not tell me much about the previous owner or where the car came from. There were no plates and no recent inspection on it, but I did not care. The title proved ownership and that was all I thought I needed. I remember him telling us he put a paper plate in the back window and that it should be enough to get us home since it was too dark to see the writing on it at night. After that, we would need to get the car registered immediately; otherwise, we could get a serious fine.

With no particular guidance coming from my home, I did not listen too closely to the warning. Had the guidance come from my mom at this point in my life, I probably would have ignored it. Besides, I could not register the car if I wanted to. To register a car in New York State, it must be insured. And I could not insure the car until my mom got back from Egypt.

My older brother and I took turns driving the car. It was much better looking than my mom's car. We could also rack up miles on my car without having to answer any questions from my mom.

Up until then, I still had not passed my road test. I was driving my car without a license, any insurance, or registration. My older brother told me things would be OK as long I had the title to show. This was one of those times when I wish I had not taken my older brother's advice.

I continued to drive the car to and from work over the summer. It really did make getting to work a little more fun. I could pull up in the parking lot for my job—no more waiting for trains or one-mile walks from the subway to the aquatic center where I worked. Life with my car felt sweet.

The other idea my older brother had was to make sure whenever one of us left the car to make sure to take the title with us. If someone broke into the car and found the title in the glove compartment, then they could transfer ownership without our permission since we hadn't registered the car. We made it a habit to remove the title and bring it up to the apartment after one of us finished driving the car.

One afternoon on my way to work, I got stalled in heavy traffic. I looked to my right and noticed there was a traffic officer giving a ticket to an illegally parked car. Within a couple of minutes, a police van rolled up behind me and signaled for me to pull over. With nowhere to run, I pulled over.

Four officers got out of their car. They routinely asked for my license and registration. My older brother's driver license had just come in the mail the week before. When you pass your road test in New York City, the DMV gives you a receipt as verification that you can use with your learner's permit as proof that you passed your road test until your driver's license arrives in the mail. The receipt is usually good for weeks after the driver's license arrives. So, my older brother gave me his permit and receipt to use in the event I got pulled over while I was driving. I had also gotten away with acting as him with his ID before. Unless someone stared at the ID closely, they would assume we were the same person.

I gave the officers my older brother's ID and the receipt as proof that I passed my road test. I went in to reach for the title in the glove compartment and noticed the title was not in there. My older brother had used the car last and I forgot to bring the title with me before I left in the car. My heart started to race a little faster. I tried explaining to the officer that I had just purchased the car and I left the title in the apartment.

The explanation did not go over so well. They asked me to leave the vehicle so they could search it. As I got out, they handcuffed me and I left my wallet on the roof of the car. Picture the situation: a 6'1 African-American male. They concluded the odds were that I was lying. I was, but not fully. They thought I had stolen the car.

Then one of the other officers grabbed my wallet. It was one of the moments when you think that things could not get any worse – and they did. The officer rifled through my wallet and found other IDs that had my actual name and photo on them. He quickly showed them to the other officers. Again, I was asked to explain. I told them it was my older brother's ID. At that point I had very little credibility. They did not believe a thing I said. They even told me I could be charged with identity theft.

I was confused. I didn't know why they had pulled me over. Yes, my car did not have plates on it, but neither do the new cars people buy, or the ones from the dealerships when your car is being repaired. When I was put into the paddy wagon, I realized I left my cellphone in the car.

It was in that moment when I realized how reliant we are on our technology. I could not even remember my boss's phone number to call and tell her I would not make it to work because I had been arrested by the police.

If I could use one word to describe how I felt in that moment, it would have been 'bummed.' As crazy as this sounds, I was excited I was getting arrested. I was 17-years-old and had not spent a day in jail yet. By now, most of the kids in my neighborhood had spent at least a day or two in jail. When they got out, everyone huddled around them to listen to them tell their jail stories. I was finally going to get my chance. I was just bummed it was happening as I was on my way to work. Why couldn't this happen on my day off, I thought?

When they finally got me to the precinct, I called my older brother to come and bring the title over. I was hoping because he was 18, they would let me leave with him. He brought our friend Turtle along; he was only a couple of months away from turning 21. I thought when they got there and proved I owned the car, the police would have no reason to keep me locked up. They would have to let me go.

I saw my brother and his friend Turtle come from the holding cell in the back of the precinct. Within a few minutes, my older brother signaled to me that the police would not release me. That is when the fun began. I was on my way to jail.

Locked up and not feeling cool

After the officers arrested me, they started to act like we were friends. They asked me if I wanted Burger King on their lunch run and one of them even ran back to the car to get my cell phone so I could get the number for my boss. They asked a few questions about the drug trafficking in the neighborhood and then they sent me back to the cell.

That's where I met the other folks who were arrested in the neighborhood that day. Two people got pulled over because they ran a stop light. When the officers searched their cars, they found cocaine in the vehicle. Another kid was in jail because he got caught spraying graffiti.

Then the waiting game began. We all got fingerprinted and just hung out in our cells. I had not had anything to eat all day. I was very familiar with what was about to happen because I had heard about this process over a dozen times from my older brother and my friends.

We waited. And waited. And waited some more. Apparently, there was a back-up at the central booking and they were not making trips throughout the day. I got arrested around 11 am and we did not leave the precinct until 8 pm or 9 pm that evening to head to the local jail. In my case, it was in Kew Gardens, Queens.

The police handcuffed us all together and walked us out of the station into the police van. Up until that very moment, I had no idea what I was going to jail for. I proved that I had not stolen the car and I did not commit any identity theft.

We rolled into the central booking around 10 pm. A handful of us were being transported from my precinct and we shared a single chain of handcuffs. We must have looked like a scene out of a prison break movie.

When we arrived, they fingerprinted us again. They took our mug shots and then stripped us of our personal belongings. They also took my belt and shoelaces. Apparently, people would use their shoelaces and belts to inflict harm to themselves and others around them. Then we moved into the second cell.

The second cell was a holding area where everyone who had committed a crime and been brought into the central booking in the last two hours was sent. There were probably fifty other people around me at the time. That was when I spotted food.

There were sandwiches scattered all around the cell – except no one was eating them. That is when I realized they were all peanut butter and jelly. Before I got to jail, I knew they served two types of sandwiches: cheese and peanut butter and jelly. The cheese sandwiches were the safest bet. I had been coached in advance to avoid the peanut butter and jelly at all costs. The peanut butter was supposedly so dry that the bread would stick to your gums and the jelly was incredibly acidic.

I decided not to eat that night. After an hour or so in the second cell, a detective came up to me from outside and asked me for all of my personal information, including everywhere I lived my entire life. When I tried to get some answers from him about why I was here, he told me he did not know.

After the second cell, I was transferred into a third cell. This is one of the more important cell transfers. The next cell is either going to be an adult misdemeanor, adult felony, adolescent misdemeanor, or adolescent felony cell. After what felt like two hours in the second cell, I was transferred to the cell for least serious offenses.

I was relieved. Almost fifty people in a cell sharing one toilet without any privacy was gross. And someone had just dropped a number two. Again, not knowing what I was potentially still in jail for, I did not know which cell I would be moved to next. I was 17, so I figured it would be an adolescent cell—but I did not know if it was going to be for a misdemeanor or a felony.

The third cell was where I started to freak out a bit. This one was a little smaller than the last one. There were only three other kids in there with me. One was charged with possessing more than a pound of weed and the other two for beating up a kid and stealing his iPhone.

When I got to this cell, time started to move a little slower. By this point, I was hungry and sleep deprived. There were no windows in my cell and there was no clock. In the room there was one sign that read that breakfast was served at 4 am and 6 am daily and one telephone. After everyone in the cell exchanged a few pleasantries and stories, we all became incredibly quiet.

Then we started to make calls. I called my older brother every once in a while, just to check in and see what time it was. I vividly remember the air conditioning blasting that summer. I couldn't imagine that I would one day get to jail and be freezing cold. If anything, I thought that it would be the opposite, since having central air was expensive.

About halfway through the night, I stood up and grabbed the cold steel bars of the jail cell. This was real. I was in jail. And I could not leave because I wanted to. It was in that very moment that I realized how much I took my freedom for granted. One of the biggest human tragedies is that we often have to experience the absence of something to appreciate its existence.

I stayed up most of the night. There were only benches in our cell and I was too hungry to fall asleep. I kept waiting for breakfast to be served at 4 am. Then 4 am came and breakfast did not. I figured they were running behind. Then 5 am came and breakfast did not. An hour behind is normal in jail. Then 6am came and breakfast did not. I started to become frustrated, but there was nothing I could do. No one would care about me being hungry. I was a criminal.

Finally, between 7 am and 8 am they came around with breakfast. They gave me two frozen plums, a box of Wheaties, a milk carton, and a fork. I rubbed the plums between my cold hands with hope that I could use the friction to defrost them. It worked. Then I opened the milk carton and it smelled horrible. I double checked the expiration date and it had not expired. I figured they must have kept the milk out in the sun or something before they stuck it in the freezer. I was too hungry not to consume the milk. So I opened the carton from both sides and dumped the Wheaties in the milk to mask the taste a little bit. I shoveled the cereal in my mouth as fast as I could with the fork they gave me.

The next cell was the final cell before I would see the judge. I got transferred to that one around 10am. They asked me if I had my own lawyer or if I wanted a public defender. I opted for the latter. A little while after, a young Black woman called me over and told me she was going to be my defense attorney. She read me what the police recounted. The police said they saw me driving without a seatbelt so they pulled me over. Then I gave them my older brother's ID and told them it was mine. After they searched the car, they found a paper plate in the back and when they confronted me about it, I told them I had gone online and printed it myself so I could drive my car around.

I was shocked. More than half of the story was untrue. If you were in my position, knowing that you were driving uninsured, unregistered, and unlicensed, don't you think you would remember to put your seatbelt on? I had mine on. The ID part was true. I also told my defense attorney that she had to be crazy to believe the last part too. Even if I did go online and print this plate out, do you think I would admit that and self-incriminate? If I was going to incriminate myself, I would do it with the truth.

My public defender seemed powerless. There was not much that she seemed able to do. Truth be told, I was probably one of thirty cases for her that day. I should have been grateful that I had representation at all.

Within an hour, I was lined up to see the judge. The judge reviewed my case and charged me with two traffic violations. They totaled about five hundred dollars when you included the court fees. Against my older brother's advice, I accepted the charges instead of pleading not guilty and having to do community service. I felt like I had my fair share of humiliation at that point.

Unlike my childhood friends, I did not leave jail feeling like I was a little bit cooler for having had that experience. Instead, I was ashamed. The experience did not change who I was, but it played a role in shaping who I was becoming. I had a new view of the American system of justice. It wasn't truly interested in the truth, the whole truth, and nothing but the truth. In many ways, unfortunately, it resembled a bureaucratic machine geared up to rake in money from people whose only other option was to go to jail. I own responsibility for not following the registration laws of New York. But I learned in the process that my arrest was made to feed the system more money and help the police achieve a monthly quota.

I started college at Baruch the week after I got out of jail. My biggest saving grace was that I made it to college without a felony or a misdemeanor on my record. I have a handful of childhood friends who were equally capable or more capable than I was, but they were not as lucky. By the time they were 18, they had several misdemeanors or had been charged with felonies. Their prospects were shot. Mine were just beginning. I counted my blessings, reflected on my lessons, doubled down on my faith, and moved forward with the past behind me.

Lesson 1: Education Can Save Your Life

An investment in knowledge pays the best interest. – Benjamin Franklin

My college education transformed my life. I know what the naysayers are out there saying: it is expensive; it is a waste of time; there are people who are unemployed after they graduate, et cetera, et cetera. While I agree that college is not for everyone, I disagree with the notion that college is not for those who grow up poor or who are marginalized. In fact, I would argue that it can have the greatest impact on those who come from marginalized communities.

My entire childhood, people would come into my classrooms and ask my friends and I to raise our hands if we were going to college. We would all look around the room and then subtly raise our hands. In primary school, we did it because we knew it would make our teacher's happy. In middle school we did it because everyone else was doing it. In high school, we did it because we were trained to do it. Nonetheless, what you say you will do and what you actually do are not always one in the same.

Why college?

After years of raising my hand, I had the recurring feeling that college just might be my best way out of my circumstances. While I could not point to too many people who had gone to college in my immediate circle and achieved success in life, I knew that the successful people in this world had gone to college. By the time I became a senior, the question transitioned from "if" I was going to college to "where" I was going to college.

I spent hours at the college office at my high school learning about different colleges and applying for scholarships with the hope that I could get in, learn a lot, graduate, and get a great job. What I did not know at the time was how much more I could get from college beyond just a great job.

Education saved my life. I would not be where I am today if I had not taken school or classes seriously. With that said, not everyone around me did. Sometimes I wonder why I did or how I did it. I hate to think that luck was at play, but a small part of it was sheer luck. As I've mentioned, I had over sixty absences when I was in 7th grade. I did not understand why I had to go to school. I hated homework and I did not feel like my teachers even knew who I was. Somehow, I managed to advance to the next grade.

Eighth grade was a little different for me. I found a group of kids I liked hanging out with. They happened to be the smarter kids in my grade. They started to look out for me. They let me copy their homework assignments and we would help each other during the tests. Before I knew it, I had stellar grades my last year of middle school.

Unfortunately, most high schools make their decisions to accept or reject you based on seventh grade performance. As a result, I wound up at my zoned high school – Long Island City High School. The high school had about 4,400 students there and a school building that spanned the entire block. Because I did well my senior year of middle school, they put me on the honors track at the high school. Had they looked at my seventh-grade performance to determine the classes I was going to take, I would have been in the classes where learning was even more scarce.

I also had the good fortune of going to the same high school as my older brother. Though subtle, it made a difference. I was naturally inclined to join a sports team and by the time I graduated, I had been on the football and basketball teams. My willingness to share my homework and answers with my teammates helped my popularity. It also meant that I was not going to get bullied for doing well in school. If I stopped doing my work, the entire team was doomed.

Nonetheless, the social pressure to conform and not do well in school was huge. It took an inordinate amount of self-discipline to resist succumbing to what others were doing. Today, I know I made the right decision. If I knew I would be where I am now if I focused and worked hard in school, the decision would have been even easier. The work would have been just a little more bearable.

I started my freshman year at Baruch College. I knew growing up that I was going to be a basketball player, a rapper, or a business man. Despite my hard work in the gym, I did not get ranked in basketball or football while I was in high school. And depending on how you look at it, fortunately or unfortunately, I could not spit bars to save my life.

I ultimately went to school to study business. Going to college was the best investment I could have made. If you are already rich or your parents are billionaires or you are expecting to inherit $5 million or more by the time you're 25, you can skip this lesson. If you are like most of America, then that will not happen for you. Keep reading.

My freshman year of college at Baruch was nothing short of incredible. I met kids who grew up all around New York City and beyond. While the classes were not as easy as they were in high school, I found that if I studied appropriately, I could excel. I realized that studying business was broader than my narrow definition of "business."

My classmates were talking about things like internships and work study. They were studying Marketing, Accounting, Management, and Finance —all things that exceeded my initial understanding of what impact I could have on our society by understanding the fundamentals of business. I met kids who grew up in middle-class households and in upper-class households.

I started to make friends who grew up in all sorts of circumstances, were of all different races, and who were studying everything from animal science to mechanical engineering. My first year of college was the first time I understood how powerful a network could be. If I ever had my own kid who wanted to be a doctor or a lawyer, I no longer had the pressure of feeling that I had to know everything about being a doctor or lawyer. I now had friends who were going to be doctors and lawyers, and maybe, just maybe, when I called them one day and told them that my kid wanted to be like them, they would talk to my kid and give him/her career advice so he/she could succeed.

The moment I recognized the power of having an established network of college-educated people, I also realized how much my own network is lacking. I, unfortunately, did not have parents who were college educated. They could not pick up the phone in the same way I envisioned myself doing for my kids one day.

As I started to feel bad for myself about all of the things I did not have compared to the kids I was in school with, I could not help but feel even worse for my friends and other kids who were growing up just like me who were not in college or planning on going to college. The gap in their network would be far wider than the gap in mine. I do not know where the assumption I made that I would one day have kids came from, but it just was a part of my thinking. From the very beginning, I saw making friends in college about being something much larger than myself.

I also had my first semi-serious relationship and heartbreak during my freshman year. While I was not fully out of the house, I felt a greater sense of independence and control over how I spent my time. I had a love affair that lasted a few months with a girl who was in and out of another relationship. My ego was bruised when she ultimately decided to stay with her boyfriend of four years. I learned to stay away from women in difficult situations like that.

Within a few weeks, I realized that my ambitions were not as big as those of my harder working-classmates. But within a few months, I noticed my ambitions swelling larger and larger, partly because of my competitive nature and partly because of my lack of exposure to what was possible before I got to college. With a 4.0 GPA my first semester, I had a suspicion that I could aim higher.

The journey to Cornell

The desire to realize bigger dreams was exactly how my journey to Cornell started. In the moment I arrived at that juncture, I noticed something else about a lot of my classmates. Many of the ones who were self-assured and sounded like they had crisp plans for what they were going to do for their lives during the first week of school started to look a bit disheveled. Many of them started switching majors and changing their plans.

For one of the first times, I felt a sense of relief. I was not as far behind as I thought I was. I also felt like it was okay to change and develop how I wanted to spend my time post-college. As long as I had a plan that sounded fancy when people asked, I did not really have to know how I was going to spend that time.

More importantly, if I was going to change majors and continue to change my mind, then I should probably change schools. While Baruch was a well-regarded college in NYC for teaching business, it was not really well known for anything else. I made my decision to go to Baruch because of my initial interest in business. But what if I decided I would no longer want to study business? Would my degree from Baruch lack credibility? That is when I learned that I should have applied to and gone to the best overall school I could possibly get into and not the best school for my major.

During the process of transferring, I started to double down on applying for scholarships again. I worked to build relationships with professors who would later become friends and advocates of my work as an adult.

I also learned about the real disparities in education. I read studies about how kids from low-income communities have lower expectations set for them, how many of them undermatch in the process of applying to college by applying to more safety schools (ones I would definitely be admitted to on the basis of my grades and standardized test scores) and not ones that will stretch them a little. I learned how kids of immigrants only had a one in 10 chance of graduating from college over a six-year period.

As the adversity I was researching became more evident to me, so did my appetite to defy the odds. When I was 18, I thought to myself that I would not only graduate, but I would become a role model that others could look up to. I would set the highest expectations for myself and achieve them so that others would have a bar to aspire to reach and exceed. And lastly, I would measure my success not by how much money I made, but by how many other people I could help achieve success.

When I first told my mother I was going to Cornell, I never would have anticipated her reaction. In hindsight, it made complete sense. My mother had never heard of the school. It was at least four hours away from home, which meant I would no longer be living at home. Her first reaction at the time was "what is wrong with the school you are currently attending? You are just trying to run away from our problems!"

While I could not give what she said any merit at the time, there was definitely some accurate insight in that statement. She was going to lose a source of income and one of her more reliable sons would be farther away from home. In my case, I could no longer keep up with the stress and the pressures of living in a tiny two-bedroom apartment as a family of six. Two of my brothers and I shared a 70-square-foot room that was shaped like a box.

There was little I could do without a high paying job to improve the situation and circumstances that my family was living in. I thought by leaving, I could at the very least free up some space. I felt a sense of guilt leaving, but I also felt a sense of guilt by staying.

Welcome to Cornell

When I got to Cornell, for the first time in my life I felt like a true minority. While I self-identified as being African American as a kid, it was not until I got to Cornell that I was truly in a minority. The majority of the kids I grew up with and went to school with were Black, Latino, or Southeast Asian. At Cornell, all these groups were in the minority. Even as a collective, we were still the minority.

I started to learn and understand privilege and, in particular, white privilege in a way I was not previously exposed to. I started to see wealth creation in a new light as I met some of the descendants of America's wealthiest families. The spaces I studied in were nicer, the facilities were beautiful, and the professors seemed to be smarter and better paid. The resources I had access to were beyond the scope of my wildest imagination. I met with dozens of CEO's of companies, the top companies in the world came and presented to my classmates, and I had access to some of the brightest professors in academia.

In the three years I spent at Cornell, I accrued more social and intellectual capital than I had my entire life. In fact, I learned to see beyond financial capital. I saw phrases such as "your network, determines your net worth" in a different light. While I had some challenges throughout my Cornell years, I loved every moment of it. While the experience of being a minority was uncomfortable at first, I started to appreciate differences between people a lot more.

I joined and led organizations like Black Students United and connected to my Egyptian diaspora in a way I had never before. The experience at Cornell shed light into why people self-segregate and the complexities of co-existing with people who are not like you from racial and economic perspectives. Despite those challenges, I grew to see opportunities as well. This was my chance to learn the rules of the game. How did those kids and their families achieve their success?

Learning the rules of the game

I learned about the importance of fitting in and standing out simultaneously. I learned how much easier life could be if you made the right friendships and treated people with respect and kindness. I learned how to lead in moments of discomfort, how to overcome conflict, and how to be a leader of all people – not just my people.

At Cornell, I was pushed to once again dream bigger and aim higher. Again, I found my ambitions swelling. I was committed to leaving a positive legacy on our world. The kids, on the whole, were smarter than they were at my high school and at Baruch. On average, they worked harder and with a different level of intensity than those I grew up with.

Moreover, their vernacular was different. They used what were initially foreign words around me to express themselves and articulate their ideas. If ever there was a place in the world where someone had an idea they wanted to bring to life or a purpose they wanted to pursue, then Cornell and schools like it were the place to be.

My sophomore year, I embarked on an opportunity to leverage the resources I had access to at Cornell (classmates, professors, etc.) to improve my community. To this very day, I remember reaching out to a guy who was a mentor figure in my life and telling him what I wanted to do. He discouraged me. He told me that Jay-Z said "you can't help the poor if you're one of them" and that one of his mentors had told him "you can't write a check if you haven't made one."

What he did not realize at the time, and what I would come to intimately understand later on, was the access to resources I had at my disposal to improve my community. I knew that I already had so much more than everyone else I had grown up with just by being at Cornell. I had a responsibility to share. I raised money and got funding from awards and departments and professors for projects to improve my community—generosity I never would have imagined.

In college, I learned about jobs like investment banking, consulting, and asset management. I heard about companies like Goldman Sachs, McKinsey, and BlackRock. While I tried to share as much as I could from those opportunities, I was also confronted with the sad reality that some of my learning had to be experienced in order to be internalized.

No matter how amazing my professors were, I had to do research that expanded my critical thinking. Along the way, the friendships I built led me on journeys I would have never imagined.

To learn what it is like to be independent and away from home, you need to be just that—independent and away from home. For you to truly understand what it feels like to be an investment banker, you have to at least intern as an investment banker.

While I'm sure there are ways to develop your critical thinking, build relationships that bolster your network, get a firsthand understanding of the racial complexities in white America, and to increase your exposure and expand your ambitions to live up to your full potential, college was what did it for me. Ultimately, the resources at schools like Cornell meant nothing if I failed to use them to do more—a lot more than to simply get a job. For as long as I have air in my lungs, I will advocate for kids growing up like me to go to the best schools in America because of the sheer potential it has to save their lives and unleash their potential.

Lesson 2: Trust the Right Adults

Never let your schooling interfere with your education.

– Mark Twain

Who you trust and learn from matters just as much as what your professors are trying to teach you. Sometimes understanding who and what the messenger's intentions are is more important than understanding their message. I cannot begin to overstate how important it is to trust the right messengers and the right adults. Unfortunately, there is no silver-bullet way to know who is honest, who knows best, and who is on your side.

Deciding who to trust

One of the hardest parts of growing up in a household like mine was that the people that I was supposed to trust unconditionally—my parents—were sometimes the people who inflicted the most physical abuse on me and my brothers. From an early age, we were told by my parents never to ask them why a decision was made. The expectation was that we were just supposed to do what they said.

In hindsight, it feels like they were trying to make us subservient for their own personal gains. The result was that, as children, my brothers and I never learned to respect our parents. Instead, we feared them. Physical punishment in our household must have been the root cause of so many of the bad things we did as kids. Never in my life did I feel more worthless than when my parents would break out into their tantrums and unleash their anger on us kids.

The feeling of worthlessness was amplified every time I was in school and was taught about how parents are supposed to love their children, how child abuse and severe physical punishment were illegal, and how parents should push their children to ask questions as a way to develop their critical thinking and develop their intellectual curiosity.

We were not afforded those luxuries as children. Instead, I have vivid memories of my father kicking me through a wall of sheet rock. I suffered multiple lacerations all over my legs after he beat me with the heels of one of my mother's shoes. I recall being beaten with the whip of a donkey our parents brought back from Egypt. We were treated like animals.

Those beatings broke me at the time. But I never wanted anyone else to know. I was ashamed. At the time, I worried that people would think of me as being less than them because my parents did not love me. It was nothing short of a traumatic childhood experience.

For years, I blocked out the memories to move forward. I got really good at smiling. I hid the pain and I masked the suffering. When my father passed away, so went the most abusive parts of our lives as children. May he continue to rest in peace.

As I was writing this book, my mother recently purchased a new car for $30,000. Here is the best part. She did it in cash. You cannot imagine the shock and look on my face when I found out about this. Despite this being one of the worst investments someone could ever make, I could not help but feel slighted. When she told me it was from the years of income tax refund checks she had saved up, I became angry.

That was money from the government that was given to her to make our family's life easier. For all I know, she could have been saving that money over the last ten years since my father passed away. The pain and the suffering my siblings and I endured selling candy on school nights and weekends could have been avoided. The days of eating junk food because it was the most affordable thing was an unnecessary sacrifice. There will probably be a bit of resentment here that I will harbor for years to come. Instead of putting the money aside for her retirement or using it to support my younger siblings' college education, she purchased an expensive car.

When your childhood is filled with people who are in and out of your life and have given you no reason to trust them, where do you turn?

Start with your teachers. I know this might sound crazy, but your teachers have signed up and committed their time to help you become a successful and mature young adult. While sometimes it might feel like they are only there to give you homework and tests, realize they are there for so much more.

In fact, teachers do not get paid a lot of money. They have to work long hours to come up with engaging lessons, grade assignments, and do a bunch of reporting and paperwork. Why would anyone sign up to do anything like that?

Like me, they believe in human potential. They believe in your potential to change the world. They are ready to sacrifice and take on the responsibility of helping you figure out who you are and who you should become.

How do you build a relationship with your teachers? One of the easiest ways is to help them. At the end of class, I would always help the teacher erase the board. It seems trivial and small, but it would buy me a little more time at the end of class to show my appreciation for them and have them notice me in a positive light.

If they do not have a board, offer to help them collect homework assignments, hand out notices, and even straighten up the desks at the end of the day. The easiest way to do more when you get to high school is to see if you can help them during your lunch periods or when your classes are done for the day. The gesture of an extra hand goes a long way.

If you play a sport, turn to your coaches. While your coaches want to make you the best athlete possible, they are invested more in helping you develop as a leader. Being a coach in middle school and high school pays very little. Adults who sign up to coach do it because they love a sport and they want you to be a successful leader. They are adults you can trust.

Your school principal, the dean or even the assistant principal are your teacher's bosses. More often than not, they were teachers before they got to their current roles. Like your teachers, they care about you and are doing their jobs to help you grow up and be a kid who one day changes the world. They get gratification from watching you succeed.

When I was a kid, I did not do bad things because I wanted to be a bad kid. I did bad things because the older kids were doing them. Nothing drove me more when I was around my friends than wanting to fit in. I tried to copy what other people were wearing. I tried to speak like them, and I always tried to copy the things they were doing.

If that meant joining them in a fight, I would do it. If it meant going into Waldbaums to steal food, Modells to steal football equipment, or Black Friday shopping to steal clothes, I would do it.

Did I know it was wrong? Yes. I think kids are much smarter than adults give them credit. With that said, use your judgement when kids who are growing up around you tell you to do things that are not in your best interest.

As much as I want to discourage you from engaging in anything bad, I know how hard it is not to fit in. You have to find inner strength to avoid being sucked into serious trouble.

One of the things I wish I had done sooner in my life was find a mentor. A mentor is someone who signs up to help you out, whether it is formally or through their interest in you. They do not have to be someone who has a job that you want to have or a life path that you want to follow. A good mentor takes the time to understand what you like to do and they make the time to help you achieve your goal.

Any of the adults I mentioned earlier can be your mentors. If you have caring and trustworthy parents, your parents can be your mentors too. I am excited to one day be a mentor to my kids and help them grow up to change the world.

If I could not find a mentor, I would have been more intentional about finding a role model. Everyone can find a role model because a role model is not someone who you ever have to meet. A role model is someone you look up to and respect, even from a distance, because they have accomplished things as an adult or a teenager that you would like to one day accomplish.

Once you identify who that person is (and it may be more than one person), whether they be celebrities, former presidents, CEOs of companies or athletes that you admire, write them down.

After you have your list in a place that you will not lose it, look the people up. Find out what they did when they were kids; research the colleges they went to; look at what they studied in school; see what jobs they had along the way and try to understand what about them helped them get to where they are today. And do not worry; you can always make changes and update your list. Most importantly, your role models should be people you would trust if you had the opportunity to meet them one day in real life.

Changing relationships with changing times

As you get older, your relationships with the people and the adults around you will change. With age and time, my relationship with my mother got better. As our financial situation improved, so did the overall climate in our household.

As an adult, I understand that growing up in low-income households, not having money for food or for rent or for the things you need can be very stressful. That stress will push you in some cases to do things that you never imagined you'd do. It could make you someone who you never believed you were.

It does not excuse us from doing bad things or justify why we do bad things, but we would be ignorant if we turned a blind eye to it and did not recognize the role it played in our lives. Moreover, I would not be able to forgive and move on if I were not able to understand. While my mother still does not understand what I do, I recognize it is because of a cultural barrier that comes with being in a new country and trying to learn how a new system operates. I do not fault her for our past and am grateful for the relationship we have today.

Lesson 3: Ask for Help

The best way to find yourself is to lose yourself in the service of others. – Mahatma Gandhi

Asking for help shows wisdom, not weakness. This is one of the most important life lessons I can ever share. It is even more important if you are growing up just like I did. After years of reflecting on my journey from a student in large, arguably failing, inner-city public schools to attending Cornell University, interning at some of the top companies in the world, starting my own company by the time I was 18, I realized that I was not afraid to ask for help. In fact, I was really good at asking for help.

For years after I graduated from Cornell, people would ask me, "how were you able to make it out?" And for the first few years, I would say I got lucky. The reason why I got lucky was because I recognized the few opportunities that came my way and I took advantage of them. That is an important part of how I made it to where I am today, too.

Unfortunately, many of my friends did not take advantage of the few opportunities we had. The solution I would propose would be to create more opportunities. That way it would become so much harder to not take advantage of any.

Recognizing when to seek help

As a business man today, I thought seeking help was sound logic. Besides, every good business person knows that they should not take advantage of every opportunity they come across. Part of being able to succeed in business is about staying focused. If you jump on every opportunity that comes your way, then you will become unfocused and potentially jeopardize your success.

As such, you need to pick and choose your opportunities wisely. Well, if you had more opportunities come your way, there is a greater likelihood you will take advantage of some.

This logic proved to be wrong. After my first year out of college, I moved near my mom, literally living within five blocks of her. At the time, I had a younger brother who was a sophomore in high school who was struggling to get his bearings together.

At about the same time, a kid I was mentoring at Cornell who I had known for about three years at that point had gone radio silent on me. Had it not been for my persistent outreach, I probably never would have heard from my mentee. As for my younger brother, I would go home and see him once a week, every Sunday night. At every check-in, he said things were fine. He made every effort to cover up his struggles in school as if everything was going well. Had it not been for the fact that we shared the same high school English teacher, I do not know that he would be in college today.

Every week, I would go home, and every week, things were fine. It was not until one day when my former English teacher reached out to me and told me my brother was out for almost two weeks that I realized things were not going well. I confronted him about it. He said he would shape up and start going. Within the same month, the same thing happened again.

But this time, my former English teacher reached out to me because my younger brother had told his friends to tell the teacher that he injured his back. I had seen him the day before and he was perfectly fine. He lied to his friends and now he lied to his teacher. Shocked, I confronted him again. I did not understand what happened. I would see him every single weekend. I would ask him questions about school and how he was doing and he continued to hide it.

When I finally told him I was not going to go anywhere until I got a better understanding of what was happening, he broke down into tears. He told me at the start of the school year he was doing really well in class, which motivated him to work harder. Within a couple of weeks, the work picked up and he was not able to keep up.

As he became overwhelmed, he started to do poorly. His grades started to slip. He was embarrassed to show up to class. He figured it was not even worth trying. At that point, he decided he would stop going to school and just wait for the next year to get a fresh start. Mind boggling! I graduated fifth in my class of 526 students. I passed five advanced placement courses, and I knew half of his teachers. I could not imagine why he would not come to me when he was struggling in school.

Right around the same time, I heard from my mentee. He was wrapping up his semester at a community college. Again, I was taken aback. Last time we spoke, he had just finished his freshmen year at Cornell. Apparently, his grades dipped so low that he was put on academic probation and advised to do a semester at a community college to get his grades back up. Once again, I was surprised. I graduated from Cornell with a 3.7 GPA and finished in the top 10 percent of my graduating class. Why did he not come to me?

Letting others know what's going on

I could not help but wonder what differentiated me from my brother and my mentee. We had all grown up in similar environments. The biggest difference was that they both had me in their immediate networks. They had my personal cell phone number, I would see and email them, yet, they did not tell me they were struggling.

At first, I was upset with them. All of this could have been prevented. There was no reason to struggle in the way that they did. I could have easily connected them to teachers and professors to make sure they had the support they needed to be successful.

Then I thought back to the moments in my life when I was experiencing failure and hardship. Through the pain and the embarrassment was a sense of shame. My initial knee jerk reaction was to always hide everything. To pretend like everything was okay or would become okay. With time, the problems or the setbacks would surely have to solve themselves, right?

My second reaction is to replay that logic and notice all of the flaws in it. No one's problems go away without the courage to take them head-on. So I would figure out how to solve them. If I came to the conclusion that I could not solve them, I would start to think about who in my network could help me. If it was a chemistry class, I would go to my chemistry teacher. If it was a college admissions challenge, I would seek out a guidance counselor. If it was a money challenge, I would go to my boss.

Then it hit me. I was not as ashamed to ask for help. I started to become a lot more empathetic to my younger brother and my mentee. Fears can often times paralyze us and prevent us from acting. I started to think about how I would react if I was in their shoes and struggling like one of them.

I would be afraid to ask people because I would not want to bother them. Or maybe, people thought I was smart and by asking for help it would mean I was dumb. While those thoughts rarely ran through my head, I could not help but imagine that they might have.

Today, my younger brother is enrolled in a four-year college. He completely turned his grades around and took several advanced placement courses before he finished high school. The same happened with my mentee. He is now on his way to graduate school. In both of their cases, I could not begin to imagine what would have happened if I had not been involved in their lives. I started to reflect further on my own life and goals.

Asking for help is not only a skill that we need to succeed in school. It is a skill we have to master to succeed in life. Time and time again, I would see incredibly successful people talk about how they got to where they are and they would pause to say that they did not do it alone.

In fact, there were dozens of people along their entire journey who stepped up and provided them with guidance, mentored them through challenging times, and opened doors for them. I would also say the same is true for me.

How do you get the support you need? You ask for it. In school and in the work place. When people step up to help you, do everything in your power to be prepared to make sure they feel that it was worth their time.

Poverty and the ability to ask for help

At first, I thought I stumbled upon why middle class and affluent kids were more likely to succeed than students mired in poverty. It had to be because middle class and affluent kids were better at asking for help. Anecdotally, though, I knew that it was not true.

However, I did notice that middle class and affluent kids did not have to ask for help as often. That is because there were social constructs in place that made it less likely for them to have to ask. Compared to low-income students, middle class and affluent students were more likely to go to better schools, to have more engaged parents who understood the school system, and to have been college educated and possess networks that could help accelerate their children's careers. In the same way I would reach out to my younger brother and my mentee, more caring adults may surround a kid who is growing up middle class or affluent, which would prevent them from slipping through the cracks.

I came to the conclusion that middle class or affluent kids are no more likely than a poor kid to ask for help. Kids being raised in a more affluent socioeconomic group are still kids. They are likely to exhibit many of the same fears of asking someone for help, wasting someone else's time, being perceived as dumb, and so forth.

The largest difference appears when a child is struggling. In a middle class or a more affluent household, if a kid is struggling, there is a greater likelihood that someone will come to their rescue and make sure they receive the support they need, even if they do not ask for help. However, in a low-income household, if a kid does not ask for help, there is a strong likelihood that no one will help him or her.

Ultimately, we all struggle. We all have moments when we need someone to pick us up. It is up to us if we choose to struggle on our own or if we reach out for support. As a society we need to do a better job teaching that asking for help is not a bad thing and is, in fact, one way to succeed.

Lesson 4: The Secret to Success is Less, Not More

Only once you give yourself permission to stop trying to do it all, to stop saying yes to everyone, can you make your highest contribution towards things that really matter. – Greg McKeown

One of the most important lessons I have ever learned in my life is that the secret to being successful is about doing less, not more. When I first learned this secret, I did not believe it could be true. While it may appear that I have my hands in a lot of different things, the truth is I can count on one hand the number of things that I am meaningfully engaged in.

In fact, I was 22 and I was sitting down with one of my mentors eagerly telling him about all of the success I had building my company. Within minutes, I started telling him about a franchise I was getting ready to launch, an investment collective I was going to help expand, an idea for a technology company I was working on, the different fellowships I had taken on, and the social networks that I was going to join in NYC. Throw in the family obligations I took on after college, my desire to maintain an active lifestyle, and I was in way over my head.

Running one company well is better than running two or even three companies poorly. Additionally, having more companies does not increase your likelihood of succeeding at any one of them.

Focusing on reachable goals

At this point, I had been engaged with my current company for a little over three years. We had received traction and a bit of publicity, but we were nowhere near our fullest potential.

Today, more than 80% of my time and attention is focused on Practice Makes Perfect and it feels right.

After almost ten minutes of me rambling about all of the things I was doing, my mentor (who sat there patiently listening to all of the things I was working on or going to be working on) directed my attention to one of the most valuable leadership lessons I've learned in my life: the disciplined pursuit of less.

Socially, it is actually harder to do less than it is to do more. I do not fully understand it yet, but it is much harder for us to say no to things in life than it is to say yes. The only problem with saying yes to everything is that you have to do it. If you have ever done anything really well in your life, it has usually happened when you were laser focused on that one thing. If you have not, then try it. If you believe you have done something super impressive without being laser focused, I want you to imagine how much better it could have been or your future undertaking could be if you were laser focused.

The disciplined pursuit of less is an essentialism theory that was coined by Greg McKeown. Simply framed, success is our biggest barrier to becoming very successful. I recall not being able to fully wrap my head around how simple the idea was at the time.

Success is our biggest barrier to becoming very successful. How could that be? Doesn't success breed success? If so, then if you started succeeding, you should over time continue to become more successful, right? This made a lot more sense to me as I started to think about athletes and celebrities whose lives were always in the spotlight. It is rare to see a player in the NBA or even the NFL who is successful and talked about it for more than five years straight. People like Michael Jordan, Kobe Bryant, LeBron James and Tom Brady are exceptions.

By the end of our lunch, my mentor directed me to one of McKeown's articles and his book. Like most 22-year olds, I did not want to hear information that contradicted my views on the world. Besides, I was already moving forward with a lot of the commitments I mentioned earlier. To make matters worse, I had already gotten other people to join these commitments with me. I had inspired them into action. If I pulled out or pulled away, then I would be letting them down. I was more uncomfortable with the prospect of letting other people down than I was with the prospect of failure at that point. I was experiencing the social pressure associated with saying "no" firsthand. And it was uncomfortable.

It was not until a couple of months later when I started to notice a dip in the quality of my own work, and my first company starting to hit a wall when I realized that something had to change. If not, I risked letting everyone down, including myself. That stark realization was direr than letting a few people down who had invested a couple of months of time and energy. In my primary business, people had committed years and tens of thousands of dollars at that point. I owed them my undivided attention. That is when I uncovered the Greg McKeown article I was supposed to have read months ago. It started to make a lot more sense. The ideas were crystal clear at that point.

McKeown's rationale is summed up into four phases:

Phase 1: When we really have clarity of purpose, it leads to success.

Phase 2: When we have success, it leads to more options and opportunities.

Phase 3: When we have increased options and opportunities, it leads to diffused efforts.

Phase 4: Diffused efforts undermine the very clarity that led to our success in the first place.

What I gleaned from McKeown is that success is all about the disciplined pursuit of less. Success does not breed success. Success breeds opportunities. What you decide to do, or not do based on this logic, dictates whether or not you will continue to achieve more success.

For a couple of months, I resisted what I gleaned from McKeown. I reasoned that my commitments were opportunities I was supposed to take advantage of so I could be very successful. Over time, however, something happened. I realized that my fundraising within Practice Makes Perfect was slowing, transparency was decreasing, and morale was not where I would have liked it to be.

In that moment, it was clear that I did not have clarity of purpose. I was over involved to be successful, but the number of commitments I was involved with is not how I measure my success. I thought all of my commitments would make me more money in the short term, but I was not living my life to chase money. Nor did I need that much money in the short term. I was making enough to support my lifestyle and then some.

My purpose was to create a more equitable education system for kids growing up just like me. That was Practice Makes Perfect's aim. Everything else was secondary. I needed to double down on my original efforts and move away from all of the things that were detracting from that purpose.

I shifted gears after I carefully evaluated my priorities, my commitments, and my values. As I went through the personal reflection exercise, I started to let my personal values dictate my commitments and I began to make the difficult decision of letting things go. I learned that I had to say no more often if I was ever going to be able to say yes to the things that I wanted to do. In fact, I got really good at saying no, too. When people would make requests of me, I would reply: "Thank you so much for thinking of me or for considering me for this opportunity. I'm actually way overcommitted at the moment between work, travel, and my family. If anything changes, I'll be sure to reach out. Thank you for understanding."

It took me a little while to realize how important it was to protect my time and get used to saying no to doing things I would have normally loved to do. Nonetheless, the concept works. The framework is tried and true. Less really is more. Success really does breed opportunities. Most opportunities are really not worth pursuing, not because they are not good, but because they detract and distract you from your initial purpose and mission.

The fruits of doing less

Less than three years later, Practice Makes Perfect is healthier and thriving. We grew student reach by 100% in the last two years. More importantly, I feel great. Are you willing to evaluate your life and make the sacrifices you need to be very successful? Are you willing to pursue less to do more?

Lesson 5: Understand the Rules of Society and Play by Them Sooner

I've missed more than 9,000 shots in my career. I've lost almost 300 games. 26 times, I've been trusted to take the game winning shot and missed. I've failed over and over again in my life. And that is why I succeed. – Michael Jordan

Understanding the secret to success used to be enough, and if you are lucky enough to be born a heterosexual, white, middle-class American male growing up in an educated two-parent household, it may still be enough. Unfortunately, if you are like me and the rest of America, then I would be doing you a disservice if I told you that the disciplined pursuit of less and focus were all that you would need to achieve the success you want in your life.

I came to this realization only in the last five years or so of my life, and it changed my world. In fact, at first, I was not even conscious of the fact that I was growing in this way.

You know the saying, "life is just one big game?" Well, believe it. The sooner you understand the game and the rules of the game, the sooner you will achieve the success you want to see in this world. Here's the kicker: the rules in the United States are different from the rules in India and are different from the rules in China and in Australia.

The second part of success involves playing by the rules based on where you are. When I became conscious that I was playing by a set of rules, and they were helping to drive my success, I wanted to understand what they were and I wanted to understand why they were.

Reasons for the rules of society

I am going to start with the why. Let's start with the history of the United States of America. In the late 1400s, some infamous dude named Christopher Columbus claimed to have discovered this new land. Despite the fact that there were other groups of people already inhabiting the land, he claimed to be its founder.

We know a lot about Christopher Columbus, but the only thing that matters in this context in understanding social rules is that he was a white man from Europe.

Over the course of the next one hundred or so years, people fled Europe and started settling in this new land called America. Most, if not all, were white folks seeking religious asylum and a better life. In 1602, the British started catching on that people were fleeing Britain to avoid taxation. The British decided to colonize America. Slowly but surely, the people of America became frustrated with their British overlords. One of the reasons they fled Britain and Europe was to avoid British governance.

For several years, the British started to engage in wars all around the world. Wars are incredibly expensive to fight. In order to cover the costs, the British would increase the taxes on its colonies around the world. The early Americans hated the idea of taxation, and now, they were paying taxes for Britain to go out and fight wars that they did not understand or agree with. This was the genesis of the famous phrase "no taxation without representation" that ultimately led to the American Revolutionary War.

When we won the war, we claimed our independence from the British. At the time, women did not participate in war and there was very little information about people of other races who were inhabiting America alongside these European descendants. It is very plausible that the Native Americans played a bigger role than history gives them credit for during the American Revolution.

With that said, the victor was the white man. As such, our founding fathers were all white men. The overwhelming majority voice in the room when the rules, both written (like the U.S. Constitution) and unwritten (like social customs and dress), were created meant they were written to support the white man's social and economic success.

As you can imagine, the rules were written by the white man. Since there was no other dominant voice in the room, the rules were written for the white man. Since this was a society that was going to create the rules, our white founding fathers had to define them in a way that would reward people who played by the rules and punish people who did not.

Therefore, the rules were written to support the white man's ascent to success. To recap, the rules in America were written by the white man, for the white man, to support the white man. Here are just a few examples of written and unwritten rules:

Dining

- Your bread is always to your left
- Your water glass is always to your right
- You should chew with your mouth closed
- Elbow should never be on the dinner table
- Your salad fork is the outermost fork on your left, then your dinner fork is to the right of it
- Your knife and spoon are on your right
- Your dessert fork is above your plate

Government

- In order to run for President, you must be born in the United States
- If you have a felony on your record, you cannot vote
- You must be 18 years or older to vote for an elected official
- You cannot technically work for a period of longer than one year without a green card or citizenship
- A percentage of your earnings must be taken for taxes that fund government activities

School

- Show up every day
- Be prepared with a notebook and pencil
- Obtain permission to use the restroom
- Pass all of your classes to play on sports teams
- Do your homework
- Respect your teachers and all of the adults in the building
- Show up for class by a certain time
- Earn good grades and you will get into a better school

Workplace

- Showing up exactly on time is late
- In a formal situation, men should wear a tie and women should wear heels
- Show up before your boss and leave after him/her
- Follow the company dress code
- If you make your boss's life easier, you will have a great likelihood of being promoted
- There is a hierarchy and it needs to be respected
- Submit a resume to showcase your previous work experience

Society

- Goods and services must be purchased, no stealing
- If someone violates a law, they usually receive a ticket. More serious offenses require jail time
- Police and the government system, not the people, are responsible for enforcing the rules
- Killing someone else is only warranted in an extreme case of self-defense. All crimes must be handled by the authorities

These are just some of the many rules. Frankly, I think a lot of them suck. Unfortunately, I have come to realize that many of them are here to stay. After all, they have survived hundreds, if not thousands, of years.

When I had my initial hunch that there was a system of rules and finally connected the dots that these rules existed, I wanted to understand where they came from and why they were written. Only then did it become easier to digest them. Without fully understanding the first part of American history it becomes difficult to accept and understand any rules.

But the sooner you understand the rules and start playing by them, the sooner you can unlock your full potential to succeed. Not playing by rules limits your potential. Understanding the unwritten rules is just as important as understanding the written rules. The hardest part is making sure that in playing by the rules of the game that you do not lose yourself and forget where you came from.

Code switching to play by the rules

One of the things that has helped me play by the rules in order to succeed is this notion of the modern version of code switching. Historically, code switching referred to people who would switch between two different languages. The more modern version of code switching refers to people changing pieces of who they are in different situations to integrate and fit in with the group. The benefits of fitting in outweigh the benefits of trying to stick out.

The most important thing about code switching is understanding what version of you is most appropriate for every situation. The majority of us already have some experience code switching. We would act out in front of our parents, become the angels that our teachers wanted in their classrooms, and then become the tough, cool kids that our friends wanted to hang out with.

In a blog post in the Atlanta *Black Star*, Akilah Richards hits the nail on the head when she talks about the difference between assimilating and adapting. I interpreted Richard's view of adapting as my interpretation of code switching. Richards says that:

> Assimilation is about slow erasure of our valid presence; adapting is about understanding our environment and making some adjustments based on our understanding, all with deliberate effort to keep and prioritize aspects of our unique self, culture and forms of expression. When we assimilate, we disappear and we feed the false narrative about who we are and what we deserve. When we adapt, we define who we are, and we consciously examine our ideas and actions about how to thrive in America, all with a commitment to affirming our own human-ness and our own worth.

I am hopeful. Despite the deep-rooted challenges faced by people who are not heterosexual, white, middle-class American males, raised by educated parents. I am hopeful because I have seen people who are different learn the rules of the game, get better at those rules and achieve the success that they have always wanted.

For example, Philo Farnsworth was one of the inventors of the television and Oprah became a billionaire through her television shows. Martin Cooper invented the cellphone, and Tim Cook is openly gay and the CEO of Apple. James Naismith invented the game of basketball, and Michael Jordan became a billionaire through the sport. Every year there are more and more newly minted millionaire basketball players of color. Lastly, our founding fathers were white, and Barack Obama, the 44th president of the United States of America, was an African American male. This demonstrates to me that it is possible to learn the rules and be better at playing and winning at this game of life than the white man, only if we are willing to accept the rules and play by them.

I have seen countless friends and others lead dead-end lives because they have chosen to ignore some of the aforementioned rules or decided against playing by them. Some did not know they were explicitly violating the rules while others did not take the time to reflect upon and fully understand the rules. Some knew the written rules, but they could not fully wrap their heads around and get behind the unwritten rules.

Nonetheless, it is clear to me, based on my own personal rise to success, that if you take the time to understand the rules and play by them that you can achieve all of the success that you want. This chapter was written for everyone who did not know the rules existed.

For everyone else who knows the rules and just cannot rally behind them because you believe it only perpetuates whiteness, here are a few other things to consider:

- Once you achieve a level of success you are content with, you can use your judgement and bend some of the rules. You can live your life on your own terms. Obviously, you will have to be ready to deal with the consequences. I have friends who are multi-millionaires and they constantly speed on the road and get tickets that they pay because they can afford to. The resume, the suit, and the tie are all nonessential if you never need a job again.
- Not playing by the rules prevents you from achieving your full success potential. You might not believe it, but there is a next level of success that you can achieve if you understand and play by the rules.
- If you do not like the rules in the United States, there are other countries. The rules in the United States are exactly that, rules to govern your success in the United States. Success in India or Nigeria or Egypt looks different and the rules are also different. It is very plausible to find another country that has rules that you are more amendable to in order to reach your full success potential.

Lastly, it is important to mention the educational context and the implications for society. In 2011, for the first time, children entering the public school system in the United States were no longer a white majority. Whites, however, were still a plurality. They were the single largest population. Everyone who is studying the trends and has been watching the demographic shifts over the last few decades anticipates that we will continue to progress in the direction where the plurality of kids entering the school system will also no longer be white.

Everyone is socially conscious of this and that the repercussions of this could be positive or overwhelmingly negative. If whites, and white supremacists perceive this as the largest threat of their time, we may see extreme forms of violence and more subtle forms of oppression. I perceive the shifting demographic as an opportunity for us to revisit our pedagogy and create culturally responsive curriculum. We have a real opportunity to reposition our schools to accommodate the differences in learning styles and foster the diversity of thought that comes from groups that are less homogenous than they were decades ago.

Lesson 6: Define Your Legacy and Go with the Flow

Faith is taking the first step even when you don't see the whole staircase. – Martin Luther King, Jr.

My biggest fear in life is not failure. I remember sharing that sentiment with one of my mentors. It was probably unprompted like some of the other random thoughts I have every once in a while. For whatever reason, in that moment, I felt like everyone I was surrounded by was driven by fear of failing. They pushed themselves to achieve excellence, do more, and be more because they were afraid to fail. They were afraid to let themselves down and everyone who had supported them in their journeys.

But I was not. Maybe it was because I did not feel like there was anyone in my life that I could disappoint. Maybe I had built a skin so callous that I was not easily disappointed. My father had died. My mother did very little to support me as a teenager and I did not feel like I owed anyone anything. In hindsight, it was a rough mindset that I could easily see turning me in a different direction.

My biggest fear in life is dying and not being remembered.

My mentor at the time, a tall-middle-aged Jewish man, lightly tapped the back of my head and said, "you schmuck, that is what the Jews call a legacy." I spent the next few days learning more about legacies and what it takes to create them. I questioned whether I was equipped to leave one. I reflected on what it would mean for me and why I longed for something so elusive.

In search of a legacy

At the time, I must have come to the understanding that life has no purpose if you do not give it one. I learned that I could not care for the traditional sense of the word 'legacy' or what it connoted in terms of money and assets. Instead, I was focused on the part I believed was most important, one's reputation.

I had an obsession with life. I started to believe everything I did not understand would never really be understood. I found myself grappling with questions like, why Earth? Why do the concepts like evolution work in the way that they do? And why was I born into the family I was born into out of all of the potential families in the world? These questions seemed to stretch me far beyond the intellectual capacity of the human mind. When I understood that I would probably never be able to fully answer those questions, and if I could that I would never fully comprehend the answers anyway, I felt a sense of relief. I reveled in the excitement of feeling like a speck in a galaxy. I was consumed by a feeling of freedom and the ability to dictate my path.

Today, it is strange that in the moment that I felt life could be meaningless I acted in pursuit of creating meaning instead of stripping myself of responsibility. Most probably, it was because I felt a sense of responsibility to the planet and my Creator – whoever he was. I could not fathom that I could be created in good health, in good spirits, and with good capabilities for no reason.

While I do not think there was one reason in particular, I believed there were some reasons I could discover. Over time, I would find the reason. In the meantime, I would act on reasons that I thought could be close. Of course, this only works when you accept these two maxims: 1) there really is no such thing as coincidence and 2) everything does truly happen for a reason.

Instead of questioning why I was here, or what I was supposed to do, I examined why the events in my life transpired in the way that they did. I began to further explore the notion of a legacy and what it really meant.

The next thing I did was one of the most valuable things I could have ever done for myself. I wrote what I hoped my legacy would be. I unpacked what a legacy would mean, to be interpreted as: what do you want people to remember you for when you one day transcend this Earth?

After weeks of reflection and years of iteration, I arrived at this: I want to be remembered as a successful businessperson or influential politician who affected social change.

This essentially meant that I wanted to do something incredibly meaningful through business or politics that would improve the lives of others around me. The moment I came to this realization with that level of clarity, the rest of the decisions in my life became so much easier.

I found role models online and in person whose backgrounds I studied to embrace their successes and learn from their challenges. I wanted to create a marked improvement in our world. Among those at the level were Franklin Delano Roosevelt, John F. Kennedy, Bill Clinton, Barack Obama, Martin Luther King, Jr., Bill Gates, John D. Rockefeller, Warren Buffet, Elon Musk, Jeff Bezos and Steve Jobs. I did not want to be them. I admired them, flaws and all. Despite their shortcomings, I believe that they left a net positive impact on our world and inspired a generation to do more and be better.

One of the most famous tenets that I later learned successful people swear by is to begin with the end in mind. Having a vision of your legacy grounds you in what you want people to think and feel when your name is summoned after you pass. Once you have a clear picture of what the end looks like, then the road and the route to the end is much easier to map. It relieves you of the stress associated with figuring out which way you're going and allows you to enjoy the journey just as much as you will the final destination.

As you think about your legacy vision and your end point, think broad; be aspirational, and give yourself something big enough and important enough that it would be a shame for you not to pursue. The hope is that if you fall short in realizing your legacy vision that you will at least be remembered positively for something momentous.

The best thing about the legacy vision is that it makes decision making less arduous and time consuming. Having a clear picture of the end made the 5-year and 10-year plans close to obsolete. I no longer found myself rejecting opportunities based on whether or not they were in my 5-year or 10-year plan.

I actually started to feel bad for people who had created rigid plans like those and believed they had to follow them to the tee in order to be successful. In college, the plans they made oftentimes came at the expense of exciting opportunities that my peers could not have imagined when they were creating their plans. My peers inevitably and blindly turned opportunities down without consideration because they had not deliberately planned for them or expected them.

The most freeing thing I found about having a clear picture of the end was my fairly simple evaluation process of new opportunities. Instead of referencing a document I created that was meant to be a static representation of the things I was going to do, I instead would ask myself, "Will pursuing this opportunity take me one step closer to achieving my legacy vision or will it push me further away?" If it was going to bring me one step closer, I would act on it. If it was going to push me further away, then I would pass on it. No matter how appealing it might have seemed to someone else. The only thing that mattered from that point onwards was whether or not I could align my decisions and my opportunities to realize my vision of making the world a better place.

The last thing you need to know about finding meaning and creating a legacy for yourself is that you control that part of your life. If you do not dictate how the story will be told, then you risk being caught up in a story you wish you were never associated with—or, even worse, wasting time searching for your story your entire life with the hope that it will magically appear. You control your life. You have the ability to try and fail and try again.

I remember feeling the pressure from adults asking me what I was going to do when I got older. I remember thinking and reflecting on the things I was good at. I thought about the things I was bad at. I started to imagine myself in the positions they suggested, but I could not see the purpose in them. For a while, every lecture I heard said the same thing: find your purpose, engage in it, and you will be happy. Who does not want to live a life of eternal happiness? After searching for years, I finally realized that we dictate what our purpose in life will be. The sooner we decide how we want to spend our lives, the easier things around us become. Happiness then comes from doing what we love over and over again and not so much from the purpose that we were searching for.

Lesson 7: Money does not Solve the Root Causes of Family Problems

It's like the more money we come across the more problems we see. - Notorious B.I.G.

It was my senior year of college and I was beyond ecstatic to have made it that far. Not only had the first three years gone well, but I was on track to graduating in the top 10% of my class. Despite the challenges and the internal bureaucracy, I had been a finalist for a prestigious Rhodes Scholarship. I am probably the only living person that can say they had an interview with the selection committee that I was not allowed to attend because of a university gaffe.

That Spring, I received a call from my older brother that went something along the lines of, "Karim, I need your help. I owe almost five thousand dollars in rent and if I do not pay it in the next three days I am going to get evicted from my apartment." My older brother was never the most fiscally responsible person. He had probably found a steady supply of money, and was able to save it by living rent-free, and undoubtedly had put that cash to a different use. He continued, "I asked mom already and she is not willing to help. I do not know what else to do."

My older brother would always ask to "borrow" money from me when we were growing up. The first couple of times, I believed he would actually pay me back. For most of college, I was able to deny his requests for money because my personal evaluation of the situation was that his needs were not that dire. At this point in my life, I knew that any money I would be giving my brother was as good as charity, without the tax write-off.

Figuring out what money can and can't do

The decision would have been so much easier to make if I simply did not have the money. He got me at a good time. Obama had just instituted the tax credit that provided reimbursement for up to three thousand dollars a year in higher education-related expenses and I had just received my tax refund. While I did not have a big financial safety net, I had more than my older brother.

I felt a sense of guilt that any kid growing up in a socioeconomically depressed condition would feel as they were climbing their way out. While my family was not the most loving, I always created an embellished image of what I would always hope it would one day become. Maybe I could teach my family members to love each other, support each other, and make sure that we were there for each other when we needed each other. After all, how I could I live with myself if I had the money in my bank account and my older brother was living in the streets?

I already felt an overwhelming amount of gratitude at this point in my life. I recognized that I worked hard, but that hard work alone was not enough to get me to where I was. There was an element of luck and I was blessed with it in large amounts. I was at the right places at the right time. I dedicated my energy to the right activities, and when I found myself in the worse of situations, I got away with a traffic violation instead of a felony or a misdemeanor. To top it all off, I was provided with a safe haven the last few years at Cornell, receiving access to almost everything I asked for. My siblings were not as lucky as I was.

I started to think about how I would want to be treated if I were in my older brother's situation. I wondered how he perceived me and how he would perceive me if I did not give him the money and he was forced to live in the streets. After all, I was given this opportunity because I was supposed to share the access that I received with my community. Truth be told, the money came fairly easily to me too and I did not fully appreciate the value it had until I gave it away. The biggest mistake I made was that I was more consumed with how it would make me feel or look than the ultimate impact it would have on his life.

I decided that I would do what I thought was the right thing to do in that situation: share my blessings and give him the five thousand dollars he needed. I went through the formalities of talking through when he would pay me back and how he would assure me that the money went directly to the landlord. I also asked him what had happened to the money he was making. He lied to me about the hardships he was facing at work. I would later uncover he suffered from the same gambling addiction that defined my father's lackluster legacy.

The high was incredible. I had never given anyone that amount of money before. The ability to do that for a family member who was truly in need was incredibly gratifying. I felt like I had officially "made it." Yes, I was a little anxious that this habit of giving away large sums of money could define the rest of my life, but that would mean I was making enough money and could be helpful. I convinced myself that it would be okay. A day later I received the confirmation that the rent was paid to the landlord. I thought life was back to normal.

Then less than a month later, I received another call. The landlord took the money and was evicting him anyway. My jaw dropped and my stomach hurt beyond belief. Five thousand dollars gone. Just like that. The intended benefit was really less than a month of housing. Up until this very moment as I am writing this piece, I was convinced that he actually paid his rent. Now, I suspect that there was more I probably did not know. He probably gambled the money and lost it and was too ashamed to admit it. I never confronted him about it, but at that point, he could not ask me for more money. Back then, that $5,000 was probably eighty percent of my net worth. I would later come to understand that the asks were not uncommon and they would continue to persist.

Losing that five thousand dollars was the best thing that could have happened to me at that age. I told my older brother I would not lend him another dollar until he had paid me back. To my dismay, he never made good on anything more than a thousand dollars. Despite that, numerous requests continued to persist well after I graduated from college. And every single time, I grappled with the same perception challenges.

Money as a crutch

It finally got to the point when I realized that being this crutch was not helping any one. As much as I could, I cut my older brother off financially. Every time he would come to me for money, I would remind him of the thousands of dollars he still owed me.

Today, the amount is trivial. But then, I never gave him more than fifty dollars at a time after and it was only for food. Despite my swearing to never give him any more money, he would later call me and tell me about his bouts of depression. He would share with me his suicidal thoughts and he believed his life was no longer worth living.

The stories would end with requests for money to buy food or get a haircut, things I believed were a proper use of money. Again, I would find myself obsessed with my own image instead of what was best for him. I would find myself thinking, "What would happen if he committed suicide because I refused to give him the forty dollars he needed for food while I had thousands of dollars in my bank account?"

When I finally set the time aside and reflected on what my obligation was to my family, I came to the conclusion that I would provide them with a place to sleep on an air mattress on my floor if they ever needed a place to crash temporarily and I would welcome them to any food that was in my fridge so they would never go hungry. Anything beyond that was not my obligation.

I would find solace in knowing I was fulfilling my familial obligation. After all, we were born in the same household by complete chance. The shared experiences we had as kids would certainly ensure we had a strong bond, but I never once felt like I did not do my part as a kid.

Moreover, I do not know how I came to believe that giving someone some money would prevent them from committing suicide. While we would like to believe that money can buy happiness, we know that it cannot. For my own sanity, I needed to uncouple money and potential for suicide. If someone is suicidal, giving them a few bucks is not going to change that downward spiral.

A few years later, my older brother and I sat down for dinner and the unthinkable happened. He thanked me for cutting him off. I could not believe it. I was so shocked I did not know what to say. He continued to tell me that by giving him money when he needed it that I was not helping him. Instead, I was fueling his hopelessness.

He was bigger and better than that. He went through a funk and he made some poor decisions, but he was larger than the sum of those bad decisions. By cutting him off, he was forced to have to rely on himself to do the things he once did for himself, the same thing we had been doing for ourselves since we were teenagers. He told me how my advice kept him away from the drug dealing and all of the negativity that came with it. I was skeptical. But he was right. Do not get me wrong, I was happy that this was how it turned out, but I was in so much disbelief that it took me some time to process.

I would later apply the same thinking that fueled my energy in starting my company to dealing with my family. I have always said that we cannot throw money at the problems in education. If a kid does not know how to count to ten, throwing one hundred dollars at him will not magically teach him how to count to ten.

We need to design the programs and solutions that will teach the kid how to count to ten. The same is true with my family. If someone does not have the money to pay the rent, giving them the money to pay their rent does not solve their problem. The following month, they will have to pay rent again. We need to uncover what caused the situation in the first place and figure out how to address the root cause instead of trying to cure the symptom.

In my older brother's case, he needed to learn how to budget more closely, cut his gambling habit, and work a little harder to make ends meet until he could get to a better place in his life.

This thinking should be applied to all of one's family members. I now know that my role is not to serve as a bank or a community lender. My job is much bigger than that. When people come for help, I need to do a deeper analysis of the problem and help them recognize the right diagnosis. Only then can we really begin to change their outcomes for the better.

A couple of years later, NBA all-star and future hall of famer Kobe Bryant penned a letter to his younger self that captured my situation exactly. Below is an excerpt from the letter that resonated particularly strongly with me.

Purely giving material things to your siblings and friends may appear to be the right decision. You love them, and they were always there for you growing up, so it's only right that they should share in your success and all that comes with it. So you buy them a car, a big house, pay all of their bills. You want them to live a beautiful, comfortable life, right? But the day will come when you realize that as much as you believed you were doing the right thing, you were actually holding them back. You will come to understand that you were taking care of them because it made YOU feel good, it made YOU happy to see them smiling and without a care in the world – and that was extremely selfish of you. While you were feeling satisfied with yourself, you were slowly eating away at their own dreams and ambitions. You were adding material things to their lives, but subtracting the most precious gifts of all: independence and growth.

Understand that you are about to be the leader of the family, and this involves making tough choices, even if your siblings and friends do not understand them at this time. Invest in their future, don't just give. Use your success, wealth and influence to put them in the best position to realize their own dreams and find their true purpose. Put them through school, set them up with job interviews and help them become leaders in their own right. Hold them to the same level of hard work and dedication that it took for you to get to where you are now, and where you will eventually go.

Almost everyone will deal with a family member or a friend at some point who will need their help. The important thing to understand is whether we are helping them to make ourselves

feel better or if what they ask for is truly helping them at all. There may be times where giving money is the only way to help and there is a legitimate plan in place to get them back on their feet, but that isn't always the case.

Lesson 8: You Cannot Choose Your Family, but You Can Choose Your Friends

Lots of people want to ride with you in the limo, but what you want is someone who will take the bus with you when the limo breaks down. – Oprah Winfrey

When I was a kid many of my friends would joke about who was "real" and who was not. "Real" was reserved for the people that we believed would be there for us through thick and thin. They were supposed to be the people who had our back no matter what happened. The real people in your circle were the people you could count on and rarely, if ever, have to question their loyalty.

Moreover, if they succeeded then you succeeded. If you succeeded, then they succeeded. Unfortunately, as I got older and wiser, I came to understand that finding people who were real is so much easier said than done. In fact, it is difficult to build deep, meaningful relationships where people genuinely feel that their success and your success are intertwined.

More often than not, you will find that people around you feel like success is finite. If you succeed, then it is imposing on their ability to succeed. The pie is perceived as limited—a zero sum game—when in fact it definitely is not.

"Karim, if at the end of your life you have one or two really good friendships, then you've lived a very successful life," one of my mentors shared with me during my trip to Cuba. I could not fully appreciate the gravity of that statement at the moment, but as I have continued to reflect on my life and grow as an individual, I have understood our human limitations.

The lasting value of friendship

The truth is that we only have the capacity for so many deep friendships in our lives. That is not because we do not have the capacity to love or to welcome people into our lives. On the contrary, I believe our ability to love and be accepting of others is one of our most powerful gifts as humans.

However, to truly build a meaningful relationship with someone, you have to be willing to sacrifice. I have always believed that a meaningful relationship requires a sacrifice of time, money, and sometimes your personal success. If you are truly there for someone in your life, it means being there for them in their moments of need and being by their side to celebrate.

While resources such as money could materialize to a point where they do not prohibit your capacity to build new friendships, time will always be your limiting factor.

Building meaningful friendships was something I truly struggled with. I wanted to be everyone's friend. I wanted to be there for everyone. I wanted to know everyone and be able to help them if they ever needed someone. As I grow older, I started to notice that as much as I wanted happiness and success for everyone else that they did not want the same thing for me.

I recognized that by wanting success and happiness for everyone, I never made it clear to anyone. The deeper friendships you try to maintain, the more birthdays, funerals, significant life events, and emergencies will come to bear upon your life—more than you can handle. Every additional deep friendship compounds those commitments.

Having too many deep friendships increases the likelihood that commitments among them will eventually conflict. When that happens, you will be in the awkward position of inevitably letting people down. More often, however, those commitments will conflict with your ability to do your work or remain focused on your personal career trajectory.

My desire to be everyone's friend led me to take my relationships with my own siblings for granted. Growing up, I was incredibly close to my brothers who were a year older and a year younger than I was. We shared everything, including our clothes, our room, and our bed. I figured that is how it would always be.

As I have gotten older, I realized that, while we will always share our childhood bond, we need to put time and effort into building and maintaining a friendship for the present and future, not just the past. Time and time again, I found myself confiding in friends and sharing things with them that I did not or would not intend to share with my siblings.

The same was true of my siblings. I would see them confiding in others before they confided in me. That is when I started to realize how much more complex it was to have genuine relationships that transcended time.

Thus far in my life, I have learned that the only way to build the loyalty and the real friendships I yearned for as a kid has only been possible through a willingness to share and be vulnerable. Share everything, including your success, your time, and what you're learning.

As much as we would love to be able to share our time, success, and our families with everyone who shares our values, we do not have the ability or the capacity as humans to share effectively. The number we are limited to is usually driven by our commitments and desire to make true friendships a meaningful part of our lives.

Ronald Sharp, a professor of English at Vassar College, defined friendship by saying:

> Friends are people you take the time to understand and allow to understand you. Unfortunately, time is a huge limiting factor and thus we are limited in the number of friends we can actually have. In a *New York Times* article, Sharp continues to say that we have layers of friendships in our lives, "where the topmost layer consists of only one or two people, say a spouse and best friend with whom you are most intimate and interact daily. The next layer can accommodate at most four people for whom you have great affinity, affection and concern and who require weekly attention to maintain. Out from there, the tiers contain more casual friends with whom you invest less time and tend to have a less profound and more tenuous connection. Without consistent contact, they easily fall into the realm of acquaintance. You may be friendly with them but they aren't your friends.

While I find myself wishing that I had understood the premise of friendship much earlier in my life because of the heartache it would have spared and the time I would have saved, I recognize that I might have become too closed off and too guarded too early in my life. I learn something from almost every person that I meet, whether it be something I do not want to do or become or how to be a better version of myself after understanding them.

Today, I have two best friends—Peter who I met when I was in elementary school and Andre who I met in college. One of the most important things I learned from my relationships with Peter and Andre is that, without reciprocity, friendships can never fully materialize. Up until now, I have spoken about how we need to share ourselves, be vulnerable, make sacrifices, and be present in order to build deep meaningful relationships with others. But, I would be remiss if I failed to mention one of the most important elements – reciprocity.

Friendship as a two-way street

I remember watching movies and television shows as a kid where a kid who was a nerd would strive to be the friend of a cool trouble maker in school. The kid playing the nerd would do everything the cool kid asked for – let him copy their homework, cheat on the tests in class, and give away their lunch.

The nerd thought it was the best thing in the world to be friends with the cool kid—except the cool kid wanted nothing outside of the school support from the nerd. The movies and television shows would always end with the nerd coming to the realization that the cool kid wanted nothing to do with them and they were just using them.

I was that nerd before in real life too. Do not be that nerd. Find relationships and friendships that are built on reciprocity. They will not just appear nor will they happen overnight. But when you do find someone who is as willing as you are to build a meaningful friendship, then nourish it. And remember, you only need one deep friendship to live a successful life.

Lesson 9: Your Attitude and Perception Can Dictate Your Reality

Your attitude determines your altitude. – Zig Ziglar

"Monzer, your brother is not smart. He is hard working," said Mr. Cifuentes, his ninth-grade living environment teacher. Monzer is my brother who is a year younger. That one line changed the way I thought about myself and what ultimately fueled my success.

While it is true that growing up poor has so many challenges that run the gambit from family to financial dysfunction, there are many challenges that could be conquered if we worked a little harder. Anyone who has watched my talks or has asked me for my views on poor and minority kids knows that what I am about to advise here is the exact opposite of what I call for in every public forum.

That is because I do not believe that poor kids, often minorities, should bear the brunt of the injustices that they have been served from birth. However, I also recognize that when I speak, I am calling for a utopian world that we are many, many moons away from creating.

If you cannot outsmart someone, that does not mean that you cannot outwork him/her. That principle has been one of my guiding tenets to my personal and professional success. Whenever I notice deficiencies in my capabilities, I spend the time and put in above-average efforts to achieve above-average results. And while the process of self-development is always on-going, I give myself permission to be wrong and to mess up. I forgive myself quickly for my mistakes and my shortcomings and then I turn up the pressure and the intensity to improve.

Grasping Your Ability to Work Harder

Work harder. That is what has guided my thinking and my actions. As much as I want to wait for society to become equitable and to provide everyone with equal opportunities to realize their potential, I realize those changes just aren't here yet.

While I can wake up in disillusionment that social equity will happen in the next few months or years, I know that social equity will not. Instead, I deal with the current reality. I embrace the reality of the status quo. I work within the confines of the system so that one day I can create the change I want to see in this world.

In October, 2015, the *Atlantic* magazine reported on a study that was published by the National Bureau of Economic Research showing that getting and keeping a job is much harder if you're Black. The data revealed what so many people growing up Black already suspected: because of their skin color, they received extra scrutiny from bosses, which leads to worse performance reviews, lower wages, and even job loss.

The research study points out that increased scrutiny happens from the very beginning of the employment process because employers perceive Black workers to be less skilled. That makes companies less likely to hire them and more skeptical once they do. The companies then invest more heavily in monitoring Black employees. Since Black employees are more closely scrutinized, more of their errors are likely to be caught.

The findings suggest that it is more likely that a Black employee would be let go than a white employee for the same errors. The headline summarizes the takeaway: "Black Workers Really Do Need to Be Twice as Good."

I recognize that if I deny the existence of these implicit biases towards Black and minority people or complain about how unfair theses biases are, no one will take pity on me. Additionally, there have been several people who have come before me who have proven that it is indeed possible to defy the odds and overcome insurmountable levels of adversity to achieve success.

Believe things into existence

Every single day that I walked through the sixth-floor hallway of my high school, I read the quotation, "Your attitude determines your altitude." Every single time I saw it, I smiled. I believed it, almost without fully understanding what it meant. Today, I know it is true.

There is power in positivity. When we believe that things in our lives will be presented to us in a certain light or in a particular way, then they manifest in the way we have always wanted them to. As such, it is much better to see the glass as half full than it is to see it as half empty.

When Mr. Cifuentes told my younger brother that I was not smart, my initial reaction was one of disappointment. After all, I was striving to compete with the smart kids in my school. I was taking three Advanced Placement (AP) classes, a couple of honors courses, and I had one of the highest grade point averages (GPAs) in my high school.

I was offended that a teacher would say that about me, especially in front of my younger brother. In hindsight, I know it was one of the biggest compliments that someone else could give me. He was trying to encourage my younger brother to be like me. Because it was his first year in high school and he would be settling into his identity and he knew what I had accomplished could be intimidating for someone just starting high school, he was trying to tell him that accomplishment was just a matter of effort.

For me, it was his way of telling me he appreciated what I did and recognized that it took a lot of hard work. I earned what I was given because I sought it out; instead, of what many would like to believe, which is that we were born with a level of abilities that either make us superior or inferior and we cannot grow.

As time has passed, I have come to appreciate Mr. Cifuentes and his remark more and more. He was right. I am not smart; I am hard working. While I believe I would be hardworking regardless of the inequality in our society, there is no doubt in my mind that injustice fuels my desire to be better, work harder, and prove the naysayers wrong. But if nothing else, I am committed to acting as a role model to those coming up after me who are in the same circumstances. My journey is a journey of hope.

Lesson 10: My Secret to Happiness

To enjoy good health, to bring true happiness to one's family, to bring peace to all, one must first discipline and control one's mind. If a man can control their mind, then they can find the way to Enlightenment, and all wisdom and virtue will naturally come to him. – Buddha

Are you happy? One of the saddest realities I have come to face is that success does not equal happiness—meaning that just because you are accomplishing your goals, you have financial security, you can go on fancy trips, and you have discovered your life's purpose does not automatically guarantee your happiness.

From the time I was 18 and got accepted to Cornell until now, I have achieved a sizable number of the goals that I set. Despite that, I have always hesitated when asked the question, "Are you happy?"

At every juncture of achievement, I have received a jolt of happiness and then watched it fade as things normalized. Then I would immediately start chasing the next mile marker in a state of amnesia, forgetting that the happiness that I received faded and that the same thing will probably happen once this milestone is achieved.

Chasing happiness

In some strange way, we are all living our lives chasing this ever-elusive state of happiness. We are looking for the moment where everything feels that it is in balance; we are comfortable in our own skin, and we have addressed our insecurities. In my twenty-five years of life, I haven't found a secret to happiness.

In fact, we will never be happy all the time. There will be moments when you will experience extreme happiness and there will be moments where you will experience extreme sadness. You will be happy in times of failure and be sad in times of success. My wish is that everyone experiences more moments of happiness throughout their lives than moments of sadness.

To the extent that there are things you could do to improve your level of happiness, here are six "tips to happiness" that I have learned from others or stumbled upon. I have used them all in my life to maintain my happiness. All of them are practical and do not require much time or money. Surprisingly, the things that make us the happiest tend to be free.

Six tips to happiness

First, acknowledge that happiness is not just a mental thing. Happiness is also a physical thing. When you feel happier, your body also performs better. There's a body of research that shows that exercising for three times a week for 30 minutes has the equivalent impact of some of the most powerful psychiatric drugs that we have created to deal with depression, anxiety, and stress in our lives. We all have 24 hours in a day and 168 hours in a week. We can all afford to set aside two hours to exercise.

Second, accept that your perception can alter your mood and significantly influence your happiness. If you are an optimist like me and you tend to see the glass as being half full rather than half empty, then this part will be easy. Train yourself to see every obstacle as a challenge. See every failure as an opportunity. Embrace every setback as a chance to try a different approach. And lastly, have faith that the world is working with you and not against you.

The last part is the most important. When something seemingly negative or bad happens, instead of freaking out and feeling like things never work out for you, you will see them as a sign that the world is telling you that there is a better way or that whatever thing happened was done to make space for you to do more or do things in a different, better way. This is the mental work that I have done for myself and it has extended well beyond just how I need to see things to remain happy. It has also helped me muster the strength that I need to overcome in dark moments to achieve the end results that I have set as my goals.

Third, you need to sleep. Psychologists who have studied sleep for years have found that humans need between seven and nine hours per night to fully recover from the previous day. Having an optimal amount of sleep will make you happier, improve your memory, reduce your risk of Alzheimer's, and optimize your decision-making. You also will avoid the adverse impact of running on very little sleep.

The funny thing I have noticed about sleep is that the habits we form in our teenage years tend to stick with us through adulthood unless we proactively work towards breaking those habits. It is especially important to develop good sleep habits at an early age that you can carry with you into adulthood. I personally aim for seven hours a night. I try to be in bed by 9:30 pm so I feel well-rested when I am up at 4:30 am. I do a few more hours on the weekends. The most important piece with sleep is to understand what your body needs. We all differ somewhat in our individual sleep needs and sleep habits.

Fourth, accept that painful emotions are a necessary part of being alive. The first time I heard someone mention this, I was listening to a short lecture by a Harvard professor who taught a course on the psychology of happiness. In one lecture he joked that there are only two types of humans who do not experience painful emotions: people who are dead and people who are psychotic.

Essentially, experiencing painful emotions means that we are not psychopaths and that we are alive. Most importantly, accepting painful emotions gives us permission to be human. There is something very humbling and sobering about reminding ourselves—often—that we are all human.

Fifth, be grateful. No matter how bad you might imagine your life to be, there is someone out there whose life is worse than yours. Furthermore, when you have reconciled the belief that you were put on this Earth to do something meaningful with the notion that life is not guaranteed, you will be grateful for the simplest of things, including the fact that you are alive and breathing.

In the five minutes before I fall asleep, I try to think through three things that day that I was grateful for. If I draw a blank, I default to the fact that I was alive and breathing. I also have gotten in the habit of using my Friday mornings as my opportunity to do a gratitude meditation, reminding me to count my blessings and be grateful to our Creator for everything that I have.

There are studies that have shown that people who cultivate the habit of gratitude, are more successful, happier, physically healthier, and have stronger immune systems.

The sixth and final one that I have found to contribute to happiness is probably the most obvious: stop spending time with people you do not like or are indifferent towards and start spending more time with people you care about and that care about you.

The fancy scientific term for this is time affluence. The term refers to how the time we spend with people, specifically those we care about, and doing the things we want to be doing, versus being with people we do not care about and doing things that we do not care about.

Naturally, if we spend time with people we love and make us happy, we will be happier people. I have religiously done this with the people we have hired at my company, prioritizing time for my family, my best friends Andre and Peter, and my significant other.

Karim Abouelnaga   *BREAKING THROUGH: From Rough to Ready*

Lesson 11: Eliminate Self Doubt

Our doubts are traitors, and make us lose the good we oft might win, by fearing to attempt. – William Shakespeare

One of the best things that could have ever happened to me was that I started my own company. As overwhelming as this sounds, I believe that kids growing up in poverty are better equipped to succeed as entrepreneurs and business leaders because they are conditioned for the job.

The stress, responsibility, and the constant unexpected turns and twists of starting and running one's own business require a bit of a thick skin, experience overcoming adversity, a desensitization to stress, and comfort in a high-pressure atmosphere. Ironically, these are exactly the kinds of qualities you build growing up in a poor household.

Nonetheless, deciding to be an entrepreneur is a tough decision. If you grew up with little means, like most Americans,then being an entrepreneur may not necessarily appeal to you. But it should! You have unique skills that are more likely to set you up for success and should help you put aside any self-doubt that you may experience in the process.

Instead of approaching entrepreneurship through the lens of how to succeed with the limited resources you have, think about approaching entrepreneurship from the assets that you have lived through. Those will help you succeed. Below are the nine that resonated most with me in my journey.

Tips for eliminating self-doubt

First, force yourself to exercise a sense of creativity. I still remember the summer before my fifteenth birthday. That year in New York City was especially hot and we needed to keep our windows open if we had any chance of making it through the summer. For most people where I grew up, an air conditioner was a luxury. For me, it felt like it was a necessity. This is because I am especially sensitive to mosquito bites. When the summer rolls around, I need to sleep in long-sleeve shirts. Thus, ninety and one hundred-degree evenings could easily feel five to ten degrees warmer to me.

For days, I lost sleep and would often wake up in the middle of the night drenched in my own sweat. The old, plastic fan we picked up from the street would circulate hot-air, rendering it practically useless. I knew something would have to give if I was going to make it to see my fifteenth birthday.

As football season was about to start, I found myself at a Modell's clearance rack in front of a heat gear collection by Under Armour. The shirts were supposed to use your sweat to help you feel cooler while you are running. That is when it hit me. I immediately purchased the long-sleeve shirt to sleep in. If I sweat with this shirt on, I reasoned, then the hot-air should cool me off. Sure enough, that night, the hot-air that was being circulated by the fan started to feel much cooler.

For me, it was poverty that forced creativity. As an entrepreneur, you will be faced with an abundance of challenges without the necessary resources to solve them. When most people quit, you will be equipped with a unique perspective to come up with creative solutions to solve the actual problem.

Second, cut through noise of daily life and identify the real problem. As I have grown older and dabbled in different social circles, I have seen problems in different lights than many of my peers and colleagues. Take for example, my inability to sleep. I did not say my problem was a lack of air conditioning (though that may very well have been a way to solve it), instead I identified the problem as being hot. Growing up with little prepares you to solve your problem with little. Instead of focusing on tangential causes, you zero in on the root cause. You focus on solving the actual problem. In my case, it wasn't the external heat as much as it was that my body was overheating.

When we started Practice Makes Perfect, one of the initial reasons was to narrow the achievement gap. Decades of research showed that there were hundreds, if not hundreds of thousands, of reasons why the achievement gap existed, everything from a lack of positive role models to poor health conditions. However, two-thirds of the case for the achievement gap was directly attributed to summer learning loss.

We believed to remedy this problem, we would create high quality academic summer programs and run them in low-income neighborhoods. The obvious solution was to create summer school for all children. We quickly realized that summer school was punishment for the kids and babysitting for the teachers. Although we initially ran our programs independent of schools, we knew that the real reason why summer school was ineffective was because school principals did not have the bandwidth or the capacity to plan high quality programs over the span of two weeks. The challenge was not so much an apathy by school leaders as it was a lack of capacity.

Third is the understanding that relationships are more valuable than money. Deals are made and closed when people see eye-to-eye. When you're lacking resources or connections, you realize that there are more important things that drive meaning and happiness. One of those things is relationships.

Growing up, I valued friendships and loyalty more than I did money. As we have been building and scaling our business, we have naturally supplied that same mentality. We have rarely lost a customer because of money.

Our partners know they are more than their money when they work with us. We have been successful as a business because we have built a mindset that money does not necessarily increase happiness. In fact, we have organized our company as a Benefit Corporation to ensure our commitment is to our mission (educational equity) and the children that we serve before everything else. Benefit Corporations allow you to put a fiduciary obligation to your investors second to your mission. We have aligned our financial targets in such a manner that if we serve more students and continue to deliver high-quality programs for our school partners, then we will continue to grow.

Fourth, we are full of hope. Purpose is largely fueled by hope. The thought of possibly improving a particular status or condition compels us to continue thriving. Growing up poor does not stop at not having money to do the things you want. It also compromises the things you need. An empty fridge and a growling stomach can only be overcome if your heart is full of hope.

When situations scared us at home, like not being able to pay the rent and not having work, the hope that things would one day get better was what pushed us to continue striving.

Building a business and facing a big vision requires a lot of hope and conviction. Oftentimes, you are making decisions without any historical precedent. There are internal and external breakdowns. You make assumptions that drive pivots, and you are at your last dollar waiting for a check from a customer to clear to make payroll.

Without a sense of hope and conviction, it is easy to break down in those moments. I would posit that growing up in poverty or with challenges magnifies our ability to hope.

Fifth is an ability to focus on the positive. Negative situations and tough times are just as omnipresent in business as they are in poverty. You do not have to look far to notice that a friend or a relative is in jail or that you do not have the money for a class field trip or that the social services you have access to are not complete as those that others pay for. If you sit there and wallow in grief over everything that has gone wrong, you will be paralyzed by your anger and frustration, whether it is warranted or not.

When things do not go as planned, which is more likely to happen than not, as you are building your business, focusing on the positive will be essential to rallying your team and keeping morale high enough until the storm passes. Being a successful entrepreneur means knowing how to get through tough times to enjoy the better ones.

Sixth is an unparalleled level of resilience. Not every single person has a strong sense of resilience. More often, they will have had life experiences that knocked them down or made them feel like failures. Usually, there are social disadvantages that exist that cause a family to grow up in poverty, such as growing up in a single-parent household, being a first-generation American, enduring an abusive household, or inhabiting a drug-infested neighborhood. Sometimes, all those conditions are present.

There are dozens of adversities that need to be overcome to make it to the later part of your teenage years. Resilient people do not ask "Why me?" Instead, they ask "Why not me?" In the former mindset, you are the victim and in the latter, you are the student. The difference in mindsets can make tough situations tougher or more bearable. Resilient people opt for the latter.

Seventh is the absence of the fear of losing it all. When you have lived in poverty for a large part of your life, you know how to live with very little. Building a successful business requires taking significant risks. Sometimes it means putting everything on the line. This is much harder to come to terms with when you have only heard about how hard or uncomfortable it is to live in poverty. Those of us who have lived and overcome poverty realize that it is an economic state that can be changed.

I have risked a lot more freely than many of my peers have—oftentimes against the advice of many of my mentors and advisors. When you are at the bottom, you realize that the only direction you can go is up. That perspective serves as another asset when you are being raised in the lowest socioeconomic class.

Eighth is probably your work experience. A few months ago, I received a letter from the Social Security Administration notifying me that I was eligible for survivor benefits (if I had a family and I passed away, they would receive money from the government). That means I contributed a fair share to the system by the time I was 24. As I glanced through the earnings statement, I realized I had been working and contributing to Social Security for over ten years! I am incredibly proud of the early experience I have been able to build, and it has been invaluable in helping me build and operate my business.

Do not underestimate the value of the jobs and work you have had, even if that work is being a lifeguard, maintenance worker, or a waiter. The early jobs that are taken on out of necessity play an incredibly influential role in our professional development. You are going to be better at building a company if you have had experiences working at other places and experiencing different management styles.

Last, but not least, is what I have heard referred to as a sixth sense, which is called survival. I have heard professors and life-long academics talk about a sixth sense that those raised in poverty have. They refer to the sixth sense as our ability to survive. When conditions and situations present unlikely odds of existence, we still find some way to exist.

Not surprisingly, I vividly recall several instances when my brothers and I would scurry through the neighborhood collecting cans that were left in the streets and trash cans. We would do it early in the mornings before people woke up and on the weekends when people were sleeping in. Each can or bottle we picked up was worth five cents at the local Waldbaum's supermarket. Many times, we would want to spend this money on pizza or candy but knew we needed it to help put food on the table.

There are points in your entrepreneurial journey where you simply must survive. Perhaps you are waiting for the next billing cycle; you need to get through a pilot program; a big customer pulls out, or you need to simply get to the next month or quarter before the situation changes drastically.

Let's face it, the odds of success can feel as if they are always stacked against you. That does not mean that people are rooting for you to fail. In fact, if our country is going to continue to thrive, we need people who are going to imagine the future and dedicate themselves to bring their visions of a better world to fruition.

Growing up in poverty and attaining an education allows you to imagine possibilities where others cannot. Although these assets are unique to those growing up in poverty, challenges to starting a company are common to everyone. If we can look at the biggest disadvantages as points of leverage instead of hindrances, then we can continue to use them to fuel our success.

Even if you choose not to start a company, that does not mean you cannot and should not always be thinking like an entrepreneur. Use your upbringing to continue to see the opportunities where others do not.

Lesson 12: Delay Gratification and Think Long-Term

If you don't sacrifice for what you want, what you want becomes the sacrifice. – Anonymous

Not too long ago, I found myself sitting on a panel for AARP. Yes, the organization for senior citizens. The topic of the panel was all about breaking stereotypes and redefining what it meant to be old. As our society has become more advanced and developed so have our medicines and various forms of therapy.

Since the 1960s, the average life expectancy in the United States has gone up by ten years from 70 to almost 80 years. By the time we hit the ripe old age of 60, the average life expectancy might be as high as 90 years. If that does not excite you enough about how much you can do and accomplish in your life, then I do not know what else will.

The average person has a career that spans about 30 years. By living until 90, we can comfortably have two careers and do 20 or more years in school.

One of the hardest parts of growing up in a low-income or middle-class household is shifting your thinking from the here and now and to the then and later. We need to start thinking about the long-term implications of our decisions. When I was a kid, I would always find myself caught up thinking about what I was going to eat for my next meal, because food was not always promised, what clothes I was going to wear the next day for school because there was always a good chance I would be re-wearing a pair of dirty underwear, socks or jeans, and how the rent was going to be paid that month because my mom would scare me and my older brother that if we did not work and help with the rent that we would be living in the streets.

With these short-term pressures in our faces, it was incredibly difficult to even think about the prospect of what our lives would look like when we graduated from high school, let alone as a true adult in our 30s or even in our 50s.

Being unable to think long-term and see a vision that is 20 to 30 years out forces us into one of the biggest traps that plague people who never achieve success: the inability to make short-term sacrifices and delay gratification. This is especially important when it comes to school and getting an education.

My father dropped out of high school in Egypt and my mother only graduated from high school in Egypt. When they came to America, their immediate instinct was to pick up jobs and work. They believed, as do most immigrants and the working poor, that working to generate income is the most important thing they could do. But, what if you knew that the average college graduate earned $30,000 more per year than a nongraduate?

My mom was roughly 30-years-old when she had me. If she was to live to be 90, that would mean she left $1.8M on the table (60 years x $30,000). In fact, she could have done four years of college, spent $60,000 per year, racked up $240,000 in debt and still come out $1.38M ahead (54 years x $30,000 - $240,000). There is some opportunity cost that I am not accounting for; however, it is hard to imagine that it would even come close to the difference in earnings.

In order to do this type of thinking, you have to be accustomed to thinking long term. In my parents' case, they would have to delay the gratification of being able to earn money immediately, potentially take turns going to school, and not be able to afford everything they wanted in the short term.

In my case and in my siblings' case, we would resist any obligations put on us by our parents to support them financially if it interfered with our ability to do well in school. While getting a college education does not guarantee success for anyone, it is still our society's best lever at attaining social mobility.

Research from the *Brookings Institute* has found that the earnings of college graduates are much higher than for nongraduates, and this is especially true for people born into low-income families. In a perfectly mobile society, no matter where an individual was born, they would have an equal chance of moving up or moving down socially and economically.

However, we know that without a college degree, a child born into a family in the lowest income quintile has a 45 percent chance of remaining in that quintile as an adult and only a five percent chance of moving into the highest quintile. By choosing not to pursue a college degree, you significantly limit your future earning potential.

Children born into the lowest quintile who delay gratification and think long term and earn a college degree only have a 16 percent chance of remaining in the lowest quintile and they quadruple their chance of breaking into the top quintile. Ultimately, a low-income individual without a college degree will very likely remain low-income as an adult, whereas a low-income individual with a college degree could just as easily land in any income group, including the highest.

Higher education is one of the best investments an individual can make. To fully grasp why it is so hard for a kid who is growing up in a low-income household, you have to appreciate the conditions he/she grew up in to understand their thinking. Unfortunately, you can't decide to go and graduate from college during your senior year of high school without fully preparing for it earlier in your life.

By the time I made it to my senior year of high school, everyone around me knew and understood that college was our best chance at getting out of poverty and achieving many of the ambitions we wanted for ourselves and future families. However, only some of us were set up to go to college and succeed right away. The tough part for so many of my friends who were not prepared and wanted to go to college or the ones who understood it was the right thing to do after high school is that learning is cumulative. You cannot skip learning how to work with fractions in math during middle school and get a high score on the ACT or the SAT without having to relearn that material.

As our education system starts to focus on raising high school graduation rates by any means necessary, more and more kids will be graduating from school without the college or career readiness skills they need to be successful. My older brother is a prime example. He graduated high school by meeting watered-down math standards—so much so that he spent the first two years of his community college education taking remedial math courses, which means they were not credit bearing.

He attended community college for three years before he ultimately gave up and dropped out without a degree. Today, he is 27-years-old and thinks it is too late to go back in time and relearn everything that he did not learn. He believes that taking on any more school debt to get a degree is not worth it. However, he could not be more wrong. Statistically speaking, he has at least another forty years of his life. The sooner he starts to shift his thinking from worrying about the short-term, possibly negative implications of completing his degree, the sooner he will achieve the success he has always wanted.

Getting a college education is roughly a twenty-year investment. The sooner we can recognize the positive potential to attaining an education, the sooner we can reduce our chances of remaining in our same situation. One of the things I struggled with early on was going beyond hearing this from people. There were not many role models who were around me and succeeded by going through college. I had an innate desire to be the best. While that passion was not channeled towards school when I was younger, it luckily started to get channeled towards school as I got older. In many ways, I just blindly believed that more and better education was the answer.

Today, I am a living testament to the impact of receiving a college education and what it can do for your life prospects, especially when you are born in the lowest income quintile. While it may seem that I built that future for myself by starting my own company, I can assure you that it started before my company became anything material.

By the time I was a sophomore in college, I held internship opportunities that had signaled to me and to those around me that the financial insecurity I grappled with as a kid would no longer define me or my circumstances. The road to that point was not easy. I made countless sacrifices to get there. I skipped parties and fun events when I was a kid to study and get good grades. Now, I can skip work to explore new countries and improve the world.

The benefit of a high-quality education does not need to be realized in the first five years of your life. I am fully aware that I am advocating for people to attain a high-quality education at a time when everyone is saying that a college education is not worth the investment. In fact, everything you can learn in college, you can learn online.

Unfortunately, if you are growing up in the middle or lower class, that is not true. Yes, you can learn skills online—things like how to do accounting, math, and the basics of finance.

However, the 21st century social skills you need to be successful, you will not learn without college.

To bring this full circle, I recently heard a joke that captured exactly how you know when you are old. "The moment you fall, if the people around you break out into laughter, odds are you are not old. If they do not, and are instead concerned, then you are probably old."

Lesson 13: Follow Up

You miss 100% of the shots you don't take. – Wayne Gretzky

Whenever I speak to large audiences of people or kids, I share my email and contact information freely. I encourage people to follow up with me. Especially to students who I know I can be helpful to in their development process. The strange thing is that in audiences of 10 to 1,000+, only a handful of people follow up.

One of my early role models and mentors shared that same insight with a group of about 100 college students after he spoke with us. He went as far as daring us to follow up with him, knowing that he has dared other audiences before and they still did not do it.

I have a bit of an understanding of why people do not follow up. They might forget; they might lose the excitement they had originally; they might get scared; they might realize they do not have anything to follow up about; they might think so many other people are following up that the presenter cannot reasonably answer every request, or they might have some other excuse.

The good news is that if you are reading or listening to this book, that will not be you. In fact, because everyone else will likely not follow up, that means the speaker or the presenter who genuinely wants to be helpful will have more time for your correspondence.

One of the biggest differences between myself and those who were sitting in the same workshops or presentations is that I always follow up—always, even if it is just to acknowledge the person presenting and to thank them for their time. The only exception is if the person does not share his or her contact information or explicitly asks you not to follow up. I personally cannot remember a time where I volunteered to speak or was paid to speak and shared my contact information and was willing to be helpful to anyone in the audience and then I did not return their messages.

Because most people do not follow up when they are offered the opportunity, and most people who do follow up know that most people do not, I think there is a special affinity among the group for people who do follow up. I would posit that I do more to help someone who has followed up with me than I do to help someone who a friend asks me to help as a favor.

That is because there is something special about the person who takes the time to follow up. They have to be a little more motivated. They are clearly looking to take advantage of a potential resource. They are potentially looking to better themselves. There are the few who are just looking for a handout, but most people are not. They display traits that I admire and want to associate myself with.

There are three elements to a meaningful follow up with someone:

1. Reference something you learned from them. This requires you to pay attention to what they are saying.
2. Be genuinely interested in them and their topic. This is probably the most difficult for people who are not naturally curious. However, if you have a growth mindset and you believe you can learn from anyone and that everyone has something to share, then this becomes a lot easier.
3. Reflect and think of a thoughtful way to draw the lines of connection between you, them, and how they might be helpful to you. This element is the most important. I

am in the camp that says you should not follow up if you have nothing to follow up about. More often than not, the lack of having something to follow up about is because the reflection time was missing to tie things together.

Is it possible that after reflecting for a while, you might recognize that there is nothing to share? Or better yet, you know that there will be something especially timely to share in a week or two. Should you still follow-up? The short answer is yes. If you find yourself in that position, then follow up with a simple thank-you note. It is highly unlikely that every single person you meet who wants to help you or offer their support will fill a need for you in that moment.

As for the subject line, I usually put "[Event where we met or the person spoke at] follow up."

Here are a couple of sample messages to people I met at two recent events and one from my time at Cornell:

> Subject: WeWork Creator Camp Follow up
>
> Hi Robert –
>
> Great meeting you and Adam at the WeWork Creator Camp this weekend! Thank you so much for your time and energy! I'm excited to take your insights on our Tone of Voice to take our mission to the next milestone. Please do not hesitate to reach out if I can be helpful with what you're working on.
>
> Best,
>
> Karim

Subject: Ford dinner follow up

Hi Hanna –

It was a pleasure meeting you earlier this week at the Trends Summit dinner. I'd love to take you up on your offer to find ways to collaborate. I checked out your column on *Essence* and wasn't sure how what I'm working on could fit, but I'm looking forward to hearing your ideas.

Best,

Karim

Subject: Goldman Sachs Information Session follow up

Hi Michael –

Thank you for sharing your insights on what makes a compelling applicant for GS's investment banking internship. The point you made about having an opportunity to do a job out of school that provides you with a range of relevant skills that could be applied to any industry really resonated with me. I'm looking forward to applying for opportunities with GS this summer. Is it all right if I run my Resume and cover letter by you before I submit? I'd love to keep you abreast of my progress. Enjoy your week!

Best,

Karim

Lesson 14: Do not Dwell on Rejection

It's not about how many times you fall down, but how many times you get back up. – Abraham Lincoln

This is one of the most important chapters in this book, and it is not because it will teach you a skill, but rather a mindset. This is the reason why I have received over $200,000 in scholarships and aid, why I eventually attended two ivy league schools, why I won so many fellowships, and why I have been successful as an entrepreneur. Are you ready for it?

It is because I NEVER GIVE UP.

The fancy word for it is called persistence, which means to keep trying.

Almost every major milestone or recognition I have received, I did not receive the first time around. The first time I applied to college, I was rejected from MIT. The second time I applied to college, which was a year later, I was admitted to Cornell. When I was awarded a TED fellowship in 2017, it was the third time I had applied for the fellowship in the last three years. My secret to raising tens of thousands of dollars from friends and strangers was to just keep asking. When they said "no" one year, I would stop asking them until the following year.

I conditioned myself to believe that when people tell me "no" they really just mean "not now."

If we can train ourselves to think this way, we can unlock the opportunities that we have always wanted, but we did not receive when we first wanted them.

This is not natural for most people. It probably was not something I consciously did until after high school. That is because as people, we have been conditioned to fear rejection. We have been taught that when someone does not approve of an idea we have, they are saying they do not approve of us. That is absolutely not true!

The mind is fascinating in that way. Think back to a time someone said "no" to you, whether it was your parents whom you asked for a new pair of shoes, your teacher whom you asked to go to the bathroom, or your friends whom you asked to go somewhere with you.

You probably felt a sense of sadness. You may have thought your parents did not like you and that was why they did not want to get you the shoes you wanted. You may have thought your teacher did not like you because he/she let other kids go to the bathroom. You may have even thought your friends did not really like you.

Now, think back to a time when you said "no" to someone. It could be a younger sibling, a parent who asked you to do something, or a friend who asked you to go somewhere. During that moment in your decision-making process, did you think or say "no" because you did not like the person? Okay, maybe in a couple of situations that may have been the case. But most of the time that wasn't the case. When you said "no," it may have been because you were tired, you would not find any enjoyment in that activity, you already had other plans, or you were just not in the mood for whatever reason.

If that is truly the case, which I believe it is, then should we not take rejection and being told "no" less personally?

My success has been built on the principle of having thick skin. I understand that when someone says "no" it is not because they are disapproving of me. It is likely for a host of other reasons. In fact, if I made the same offer or the same suggestion, or maybe even tweaked my ask a little bit, and asked again, I might just get a different, more favorable outcome.

One more perspective: Do not ignore the emotions you feel when someone says "no." Embrace them. They are a part of being human. I know very well how crushing it is to work so hard on something, pour your soul into it, and be told it is not good enough. It hurts. Take a break. Cry a little if you have to. Eat some ice cream and watch a movie. Feel sorry for yourself.

For me, the greater the intensity by which I embrace the feelings of despair, the faster I'm able to brush myself off and take another crack at it. I have noticed that when I try to deny the hurt or cover up the rejection, it takes me longer to recover because the emotional hurt is being dragged in smaller doses over a greater period of time.

Now, here is a word of caution: This advice does not apply to relationships with other people. Please do not pursue someone forever who has told you they do not want to go on a date with you or be with you. The number of people who succumb to relationships because of a relentless pursuit are few and far between. You are worthy of so much more and better.

When you find the right person, you will *both* know it is the right relationship. If only one of you knows or thinks it is the right time, then odds are, it is not the right person or the right time.

Are there times when this mindset backfires? I do not believe the advice backfires, but I do believe the application of it does. You have to use your judgement. Applying to a college you have always wanted to go to makes sense your senior year of high school, your freshman year of college, and even your sophomore year of college. It does not make sense, however, to apply to transfer colleges during your senior year.

Similarly, some awards have restrictions based on your year in school. When I was in college, I applied for a Truman Scholarship which is awarded to juniors. I did not receive the Scholarship and it did not make sense to apply as a senior. I mention all of that as a way of saying use your judgement.

Finally, do not be afraid of rejection. It is a part of achieving success. I have had so many setbacks and failures that I have started to forget them because there are so many. When you win recognition for your work, rarely do they mention how many things you failed at. Imagine if every time someone got into college, they publicly listed all of the places they were not accepted. That would be weird, right?

The same holds true with life. Cornell did not mention that I was rejected from MIT and TED did not mention that I had failed to be awarded the fellowship the first two times I applied. Embrace the feelings that come after the failure or rejection, and then get back up and try again, and again, and again if you have to.

Lesson 15: Workplace Etiquette

Never leave that till tomorrow which you can do today. – Benjamin Franklin

This is the chapter that set me apart at a young age. I have my father, may he rest in peace, to thank for it. My father was an entrepreneur and as a kid I had firsthand exposure to building and running a business. I had the opportunity to interact with people from all walks of life in the first ten years of my life. I learned how to negotiate, how to price things so that the customers would feel like they got a deal and we could move inventory. Most importantly, I learned the difference between a good employee and a bad one.

That is what this chapter is all about: How to be a good employee. The earlier you learn how to be a good employee that every boss only dreams of, the sooner you will be given additional responsibilities, promotions, and eventually earn more money.

What is even more impressive is learning the things that make you a good employee well before people expect you to know them. From my experience, that age is about twenty years old. At that point, the four things I am about to share with you are expected. Just because it is expected does not necessarily mean that people do it. In fact, odds are if you are doing hourly work, then your co-workers probably will not do these things consistently.

However, I promise if you adhere to these things, you will go far. I did them and, by the time I was 17, I was working a full-time job making almost triple the minimum wage in New York City, earning more money than my mom was. I started as a lifeguard at a local aquatic center and before I left for college; I was reporting directly to one of the aquatic directors and had managerial oversight for almost a dozen swim instructors and customer service representatives.

The best way to think of the rules of workplace etiquette is as unspoken rules. Your boss would love to tell you to follow them, but they legally cannot ask you to do some of them without violating labor laws or having to compensate you with extra pay or benefits. Going forward, I am going to refer to them as unwritten rules.

Unspoken rule number one: Always plan to be at work at least 20 minutes before your shift starts. If you have to change into a uniform, then plan to be at work 30 minutes before your shift starts. For very obvious reasons such as delays on your way to work, forgetting something as you are running out the house, or some unforeseen hiccup on your way to work, this ensures that you are never late. The most important thing is to never be late to work.

When you are late to work, someone else has to stay late or someone is inconvenienced. If no one is inconvenienced, then they likely would not have you start at the time your shift is supposed to start. Why is it important that you are never late? It is mainly because you want to be reliable. Reliable people get additional responsibilities that lead to greater opportunities. Reliable people are never late.

I remember the inconvenience that would be caused at my father's store whenever an employee was late. It would mean that whoever was there for the earlier shift could not leave on time or my father would have to fill in for them until the person who was late finally arrived. I never once saw my father smile when an employee arrived late.

By planning to be at work at least 20 minutes before your shift starts, I assure you that you will almost never be late. And more importantly, your boss will notice when you are never late, and your coworkers are. This will set you apart.

Unspoken rule number two: Try to avoid all things that will make your boss's job more difficult. I am sure there are a lot of things you can probably think of that will make your boss's job more difficult, like losing a key part of your uniform, showing up late to work, calling in sick at the last minute, etc. Some of the biggest things you can do is avoid those disturbances to your boss's work life.

In order to do that, you have to get used to planning and being a better planner. It also means that you will have to miss out on parties and sometimes even hanging out with your friends. One of my biggest pet peeves as a boss is when someone requests a schedule change. I used to manage the schedule for customer service representatives. Sometimes people would tell me they were available, but when the schedule was published, apparently their availability changed. Perhaps they did not anticipate what their lives would look like.

Not only is it annoying to get a schedule change request, but then I have to go and change several other people's schedules or find coverage for you. One of the best things you can do in the situation where your schedule changes is to find someone else and trade shifts with him/her. Once the trade happens, you should notify your boss so he is in the loop. By giving notification of an impromptu schedule change, you will save your boss the hassle of having to rework the schedule. The more you can avoid the things that make your boss's life more difficult, the more your boss will see you as being reliable. You want to be perceived as reliable because reliable people get more responsibilities that lead to greater opportunities.

Unspoken rule number three: Try to do things that will make your boss's job easier. This item is a variation on the last unwritten rule, but it is important enough to be its own rule. The employees who were most successful at my father's store were the ones who would see my father lifting a box and run over to help him. The best workers were always the employees who followed the instructions they were given to the letter, like making notes on receipts and keeping them organized. Superior employees noticed the absence of the person who was supposed to relieve them of their shift and they offered to stick around until the person showed up without making a big deal out of it.

They did anything they could think of, no matter how small it was, to help make the boss's life easier. In turn, my father gave them more responsibilities and paid them more money. I took the same approach with my first jobs. When I was at the aquatic center, I learned how to schedule the customer service representatives and I volunteered to create the schedule. I would show up before my shift and I would set up the kickboards and the clipboards that my co-workers needed for their classes. Whenever possible I volunteered to take things off of my boss's plate and help her with her job.

When I got to my first internship, this mindset was engrained in me. Before I knew it, I was in the office over the weekend summarizing what was happening in the news and sending a weekly round-up to the entire office. By adding more value, I proved that I could take more on. I was responsible and I was rewarded in both instances, in one case with more responsibilities and opportunities and in the other case with a full-time job offer.

Unspoken rule number four: Say thank you. I would joke with people at the aquatic center that if they did their job right, then that was thanks enough for me. Having to do your job and someone else's job is far from fun. When you are in that position enough times, you are grateful when people just do their job. But a thank you goes a long way.

Being the boss has its lows, too. Yes, you are paid a little more, but you are usually given more responsibility and stress in the process. Depending on the job you are performing, there may be hundreds of other people who can also do your job. How much patience your boss has for you could easily be driven by how much your boss thinks you appreciate them and the job that you have.

In many cases, your boss created this job opportunity for you. They could easily take this job opportunity away from you. Similarly, your boss may not interact with customers or end users of the service you are providing. As a result, the boss doesn't get the thank you for a job well done or the positive emotions when someone is satisfied. Your boss is usually called in for the complaints.

Being grateful and showing your gratitude goes a long way, and odds are no one else is saying "thank you." So it is a small gesture that will make you appear more reliable, which will in turn lead to greater opportunities.

If you follow these four unspoken rules, especially in your jobs before you turn 20, your boss will definitely be impressed with you. With any of these rules, you have to be consistent. Not being late four out of five times is not as good as never being late. Depending on where you work, you might be surprised to find that the bar is low for employee behavior. The lower the bar, the greater the opportunities for faster advancement. Moreover, being a great employee will also help you to one day be a great employer.

Lesson 16: Hacking the College and Career Application Process

So little done, so much to do. – Cecil Rhodes

The college application process is one of many hurdles you will have to overcome on your path to college. Unfortunately, what most people do not know is that putting together a compelling college application or winning scholarship funds starts well before you apply. One of the reasons I saw so many of my friends struggle when it came time to apply for college was that they did not seriously think about college until it was time to apply to college when we were seniors in high school.

Do not be that person! This chapter will give you my perspective and a way to think about how to spend your time to achieve the best result during the college application process. This structure works well even beyond the college application process. In fact, if you are in middle school and you have to apply for high school, this approach will work. If you are in college and you are applying for competitive fellowships or jobs, this approach will also work.

Before I share my thoughts on the college application process, let me acknowledge that there are many other methods and ways to succeed with the process. This is just one way that helped me get into a great college and win tens of thousands of dollars in scholarship money.

Not too long ago, I found myself in front of a group of 7th graders and 11th graders and I gave them the same exact advice. As you think about getting into a great high school or a great college, admissions committees are going to want to see that you have good grades; you have demonstrated that you are a leader, and that you give back to your community.

As a freshman in college, I was at Goldman Sachs' undergraduate boot camp when one of the speakers said, "99% of what you are going to need to work here, you are going to learn on the job." I was a little startled because I had been in school for almost 15 years already and I still had a few more years to go.

While I understood that the purpose of getting an education was not strictly to get a job, I was not convinced that it was OK to be only one percent prepared for my future job. It took a few minutes for the sobering reality to hit me that while I could not learn what I needed for my job in school, how I did in school would be an incredible indicator of my potential for a future employer.

I started to put myself in the employer's shoes. If I was going to hire someone and I knew that new employee would have to learn practically everything they needed to be successful at work on the job, then what kind of person would I be trying to get? Obviously, I would want someone that could learn really quickly. The faster they learned what they needed to be successful at the job, the sooner they could add value to my company.

While this may not be the only proxy for how fast you can learn, your grades are definitely an indicator of how quickly you can pick things up. Goldman Sachs was notorious for hiring people out of college with near-perfect GPA's. And it made sense. If you have two people who are in the same school, pursuing the same major, and taking the same class with a professor and at the end of the semester one of them finishes the course with an A and the other one finishes the course with a B, you can make inferences about how fast and how well they each learn.

Assuming there was no influence by something other than personal motivation and their ability to comprehend the content, the student who received an A mastered 90% or more of the content and the student who received a B mastered about 80% of the content.

As an employer, if I had these two candidates to choose from, assuming everything else was equal, and I knew that I had to teach the new employee everything they needed for their job on day one, then I would hire the student who earned the A not just because they have a higher grade, but because the higher grade signifies to me that the student who got an A mastered at least 10% more of the material during the same amount of time as the student who received the B. I want the person who could learn faster so they could add value to my company sooner.

Colleges in many ways are making a similar assessment without being as explicit about it. More often than not, top universities have cut-off scores. Depending on how big the school is, how competitive it is to get in, I have heard of admissions officers putting entire piles of kids who score under a certain GPA into a pile that is not likely to be considered unless a file was flagged for a very specific reason. In many ways, how you perform in the classroom gives you the opportunity to be considered, and for schools and scholarships to look at the rest of your application.

Once you have your grades and your academics in line with what you are aiming for, then it is important to start thinking about your leadership involvement. If you are someone who is involved in many extracurricular activities, but you never take a leadership position, it can signal to someone that you are not that committed to anything; you do not like having responsibility, and people may not like working with you.

The last point is very important. At places like Goldman Sachs, they were notorious for having you work long hours and paying you a lot of money in exchange for that time and effort. This was not just the case for the other entry-level workers, but for the majority of your co-workers.

Whether someone has held any leadership opportunities is not a perfect measure for how much you may like working alongside them, it does signal that some people out there liked him/her enough to put them in a position of leadership. There were some people who worked under their leadership and trusted them to make decisions.

Not all leadership opportunities are created equal and you cannot draw conclusions about a person solely by his or her leadership role in every situation. However, I do believe that if other people think you are likable, then there is a greater chance that we will like you than if no one out there has given any inkling that you are a likeable person. This is especially important when you know you are going to be working long hours with other people.

Once you have your academics in line and you have shown that other people like you enough to put you in a position of influence, then the last area you need to think about is community service. This one is fairly straightforward: people like people who give back. Individuals who participate in their communities and volunteer show a sense of compassion and make a statement that they care about something beyond themselves.

I often say that I received a quarter-million dollars in scholarships and aid to support my education because of the community-service I was forced to do. When I was a kid, I did not know why community service was important or why I should be volunteering my time when I could be working to make money and support my family. Luckily, I found myself with teachers who knew it was important for me and my friends to do community service.

When I found myself in high school, I made friends who enjoyed doing community service and I would join them so I could hang out with them. My high school had a minimum number of hours that I had to fulfill in order to graduate. I do not remember how closely the school monitored and tracked it, but I definitely did community service with the intention of fulfilling those requirements.

Today, without a doubt in my mind, I know how important it is for all of us to take a stake in improving our communities and giving back. But I do not know that I could have fully understood and appreciated why that was the case when I was a kid. Even the simplest explanation I could share today about how we all live in a world that is much bigger than any one of us is not so simple to really understand.

If nothing else, know that people like people who give back. The high schools, colleges, and employers you are going to work for will care about this facet of your life and your application, too. Consider this new insight as your way of getting a head start in the college application process.

The way I like to visualize these areas is in the form of three buckets. The first bucket is academics, the second bucket is leadership, and the third bucket is community service. My goal is to fill each bucket up as much as I possibly can. The important thing to remember about this is that the order in which these buckets are filled up matters.

If you have your community service and leadership buckets filled, which is what I often see, and your academics bucket is empty, then you are likely going to have a hard time getting into the college of your choice. What I do not want is for a college, a high school, or an employer to be the one that makes the decision for you because you did not take the time to get the best grades you could possibly get, demonstrate your leadership potential, and give back to your community.

I may also be a little biased, but I believe if we all pursued our education with slightly more vigor, if we all stepped up just a little more to lead initiatives to improve the world, and if we all dedicated just a little bit more of our time to giving back to others and helping them along in their journey's, then we would make our time on this planet just a little brighter.

Conclusion

Everything will be okay in the end. If it's not okay, it's not the end. – John Lennon

If you attend one of America's public schools today, you are going to school at a time when our school system is incredibly segregated by class, by race, and by geographic upbringing (rural, suburban, and urban). As technology continues to foster communication and make connection with people that much easier, it is incredibly important to be able to comfortably interact with people across different races and classes.

If you are growing up poor, my hope is that this book gives you the confidence you needed to know that it is in fact possible to "outwork" your circumstances and alter your life prospects. If you are growing up rich, my hope is that this book sheds a little light on the responsibility you have to leverage your resources to do more good. If you are growing up anywhere in the middle, I hope this book teaches you a thing or two to help you along your journey.

If I could wave a magic wand and build an ideal world, I would eliminate inheritance and taxation in a single swoop—inheritance because I believe that your parentage is complete luck. The fact that one child is born into a family that has a lot of privilege and someone else is born into one that does not have much does not mean that one child is more deserving and the other less.

I also believe that if we could not pass anything down to our kids, we would all take more responsibility for the collective whole of society. When I was in college, I had a handful of friends whose futures were set in stone. They had no choice in what they were going to do after school because their families needed them to run their businesses or manage their assets that were accrued by prior generations. Some of them would have been much happier doing something else.

I would simultaneously end taxation because I believe it creates a disincentive for people and companies to continue to build and innovate. In many ways, it stifles risk taking because the payout has to be greater for people to take risk. As such, societies go without innovations that improve quality of life because no one is willing to take the business risk to supply them.

In my travels, I have seen far too many people and countries plagued by inefficient technology and suffering from problems that have already been solved in more developed countries.

Ending inheritance and taxation could possibly level the playing field. I envision a world where every child, regardless of the zip code they are born into, is able to attain up to a PhD without bearing any financial burden. I also envision a world where every person is offered high quality healthcare regardless of their social class or situation. If we truly want to level the playing field and ensure that everyone has an equal opportunity at achieving the life they want, then we need to create quality systems of healthcare and education.

What happens to all of the money that people accumulate during their lifetime? It gets reinvested in society. The people who accumulate the wealth can choose to invest in companies, support charities, schools, or hospitals. Whatever is not used at the end of the person's life could go back to the government to be used to bolster social welfare programs.

Unfortunately, I do not know if we will ever get to a day when the world I envision would become reality, mainly because of the factions that divide our society. If you are not rich, then you are against the rich. If you are not a Republican then you are against the Republicans. If you are not a Black person, then you are against Black people—all of which are far from true, but a tempting simplification of life when we have programmed ourselves to divide ourselves instead of to unite. And I say programmed because none of us is born to hate someone else because of the color of their skin, the amount of money in their pockets, or the platform of their politics. We train and condition ourselves to do that.

I am sharing these insights with you because I have not given up hope on this dream completely. However, I know as an adult that I have lost the naivety, idealism, and the creativity necessary to bring this vision to fruition. But I imagine that you have not.

I once had a friend ask kids under 16 and adults over the age of 18 a simple question: "If you could change one thing about your body, what would it be?" All of the adults said things like they would make themselves taller, make their foreheads or noses smaller, opt for bigger eyes, or get straighter hair – exactly as I probably would have answered. All of the under-16 kids, however, asked for things like cheetah legs so they could run faster, shark jaws so they could bite bigger, and mermaid tails so they could swim faster.

While it is easy to laugh at how the kids responded, every artist, musician and entrepreneur would quickly marvel at the beauty of those responses. Those are the types of answers that you would expect from someone who has the potential and the ingenuity to create. Every entrepreneur and musician and artist who has ever created something worthwhile knows that the idea of their creation may sound outlandish or unrealistic to those around them until they bring their vision to life. The reason is that the people around them cannot stretch their minds far enough to imagine what has not been realized yet.

While those kids may not be able to change their DNA to grow fins or change the composition of their teeth, they might one day create the artificial versions that function just like the real things. The realizations of those fins, and legs, and teeth are only possible because they envisioned their potential at some point.

As an adult today, I know that the kind of creative thinking needed to shape the world we need to live in has already started to escape me. The limitless potential of my mind's ability to create and imagine has been constricted by reality and the influence of older, less creative people. To reconstruct the environment in which adults would return to that type of creative thinking would take serious effort, something I could only dream of doing in another life where I have not committed my time to addressing the ailments of our public education system.

You, however, have the potential, the creativity, and the energy to change the world. In the years ahead of you, I hope that you will be exposed to worlds that you could not before imagine. I hope you will succeed in unlocking the vision you need to succeed beyond your wildest dreams. As you reach ever higher levels of success, remember that there is nothing you owe me.

Just pay it forward.

Acknowledgements

Sharing this story wasn't easy and I want to make it clear that it was not meant to degrade my family. Rather, I wish that my life story and lessons be used as tools for kids growing up in similar environments to know that things can get better. Where you are today with your family and finances does not have to be where you end up tomorrow. You can improve your relationships and your financial situation.

I'm grateful for my amazing cover designer and colleague Charles Baker who came up with the concept of the map and helped bring the concept to life.

Thank you to my girlfriend Kadaicia-loi who went through the first iteration of the changes and spent countless hours with me revising the book's structure and grammar.

Thank you to my best friends Andre and Peter who have continued to love and accept me for who I am.

Special thank you to Jorge Perdomo, Yesenia Peralta, Kevin Bryant, Elizabeth Ngonzi, Charles Baker, Stephen Reese, Fran Matola, Wendy Lau, Mahmoud Khedr and the handful of other friends who did a line edit of the manuscript.

Thank you to the many organizations that and mentors that believe in me and the work I continue to carry out. This book is an extension of your impact.

Thank you to the friends and family who read the book and provided your honest feedback and endorsements.

Lastly, thank you to my future readers who have made the commitment to better their lives by picking up this book.

www.ingramcontent.com/pod-product-compliance
Lightning Source LLC
Chambersburg PA
CBHW071723090426
42738CB00009B/1856